RESCUE SHOP
WITHIN A YARD OF HELL

The Story of BETEL

Stewart and Marie Dinnen

D0809782

Christian Focus Publications

Some people wish to live within
the sound of church or chapel bell,
I'd rather run a rescue shop
within a yard of hell.

C. T. Studd

ISBN 1-85792-122-4

Published by
Christian Focus Publications Ltd
Geanies House, Fearn, Ross-shire,
IV20 1TW, Scotland, Great Britain.

Printed and bound in Great Britain by
Cox & Wyman Ltd, Reading, Berkshire

Cover design by Donna Macleod

CONTENTS

MAP OF BOOK

In order for you to appreciate the amazing work God is doing in and through Betel, the book has been divided into three sections, with each section describing an important aspect of the work of Betel.

To begin with, you should read the *Introduction* (pages 19-24) in which Stewart Dinnen explains some of the activities of Betel. Then follow that by reading the story, found on page 13, of Raúl and Jenny Casto entitled *How Did This Nightmare Begin*. Their story shows what type of people Betel are helping, and how they can be transformed by the grace of God.

Once you have finished reading the Introduction and Raúl and Jenny's story, you have a choice.

If you want to read similar stories to Raúl and Jenny Casto, then Section 2, *The Rescue Process*, beginning on page 95, contains sixteen accounts of others who have been changed by the power of God from a life of drug addiction, broken families and other terrible situations to knowing forgiveness and acceptance.

However, should you wish to know more of Betel's growth and of the calling and vision of its leaders, then you should read Section 1, *Growth of Betel*, beginning on page 25.

The third section, *Paying the Price* (beginning on page 223), includes details of the worldwide effect of AIDS, interviews with Betel workers on how they interact with those seeking help, and chapters summarising the immense personal cost of being involved in such work.

FOREWORD

I am an old friend of Stewart Dinnen, one of our former WEC leaders. I am delighted that he, with Elliott Tepper and Kent Martin, has put together the stirring testimonies which comprise this totally surprising development in our Spanish work.

Faith always means shocks, because it causes something to happen—a release of God's power—not as a result of human reasoning but as a manifestation of his purposes for the world, just as Jesus himself was.

To me it was a jolting shock to hear Spaniards of the toughest sort becoming such vigorous immediate responders to truth. Which of us would have chosen to deliver the revolutionary gospel to heroin addicts, thieves and prostitutes, and then have expected such a dynamic reaction? It is just like the Lord to take on what appears to be impossible and turn it into one of the most dramatic responses to the saving truth of Jesus in Europe today.

I have watched for years to find men of the same quality and recklessness as C. T. Studd, and when I heard Elliott describe his approach to building Betel's centres, I said, 'Ah! Another C. T. Studd in the making!' We have many outstanding people in WEC, but few who are way in front in faith and sacrifice. Elliott is one of these, as you will discover in the pages that follow.

I leave the story to give its own details. While Studd's life appeared to many in his own day to be that of a fairly commonplace missionary, more than half a century later his story still grabs attention on a worldwide scale.

Likewise, we welcome the enduring value of Betel's 'against-the-odds' story, and salute Elliott and his increasing army, in whom the pure light now shines. WEC's bells—and heaven's—have been set a-ringing!

NORMAN P GRUBB
Fort Washington Pa.
November 1993

DEDICATION

Because Betel, through the gospel, is simply restoring the image of the Father to a generation which has lost it, we would like to dedicate this book to the 'FATHER'. Firstly, to the 'Father of lights' from whom every good and perfect gift comes. And then to our own fathers, both natural and spiritual, who have in their measure transmitted that great heavenly heart and image to us, that we might pass on what we have received to others.

We would specifically like to acknowledge the fragrance and spirit of the Father which Norman Grubb, Costa Deir, A S Worley and many others have breathed into Betel so that we, in turn, may bring forth new generations of sons, daughters, fathers and mothers for the kingdom of God.

'Yea, even when I am old and grey-headed, O God, forsake me not, until I have declared thy strength unto the next generation, thy might to every one that is to come!' (Psalm 71:18, American Standard Version).

INTRODUCTION

What an exciting stimulus to faith awaits the reader of these pages! Transformed lives, sacrificial service, miraculous provision, the joys of deliverance, compassionate community living—all these and much more combine to provide a veritable kaleidoscope of the grace of God at work in human lives. This story covers a unique and on-going work of the Spirit which will enrich and encourage all who read it.

However some basic information is essential for understanding what follows. The 'Associación Betel' was the name chosen for the drug rehabilitation ministry that emerged from the Spanish church-planting work of WEC International. (This is a large inter-church faith mission with a membership of 1,600, working in 55 countries around the world. It is committed to outreach among those not already touched by the saving gospel of Christ.) 'Betel' is the Spanish word for 'Bethel', meaning 'House of God' (Genesis 3:8).

On the Streets of San Blas

In 1983 a small group of WEC missionaries involved in street evangelism became aware of the huge number of drug addicts in San Blas, a suburb with the highest crime rate in Madrid. Besotted by drink and drugs and driven by the compulsive desire for the next 'fix', here was a group that challenged the new workers to the depths. In December Elliott and Mary Tepper from USA and Billy Glover from Northern Ireland agreed that a house meeting should be commenced on a Friday night in the Teppers' apartment so that street contacts could learn more about the gospel. They were joined two months later by Lindsay McKenzie from Australia who was still on language study. (Myk Hall, also

7

from Australia, was to join the team in October 1985.)

During the next year they spoke with many addicts and referred a number to the existing centres—Teen Challenge, REMAR (REhabilitación de MARginados) and RETO (REhabilitación de TOxicomanos). At no little sacrifice Elliott personally drove a great number of them to their destinations—journeys involving hundreds of kilometres.

In the midst of all this the Lord clearly spoke to the Teppers and to Lindsay and gave them a vision of a WEC rehabilitation centre. The concept was presented to the Spanish WEC team in October 1984, and although it was not embraced as a team project, the Teppers and Lindsay were given encouragement to pursue the idea further.

A new development — almost by accident

As 1985 wore on, the flow of referrals from San Blas to the three co-operating centres became so great that they were unable to cope, and it was at this point that the three missionaries faced squarely the need to open their own rehabilitation facilities. Then quietly, almost imperceptibly, an incident happened which started a whole new sequence of events. Raúl Casto, a needy addict who was awaiting a court hearing in two weeks, had nowhere to live, so Lindsay McKenzie offered to have him stay with him in his eighth floor flat. It was a casual offer made without premeditation, but it resulted in the commencement of Betel's residential programme, as succeeding chapters will reveal.

Since then, Betel churches and centres have flourished. Over 13,000 have gone through the programme (more than 3,600 in 1994 alone) conducted in 90 residences over eighteen provinces of Spain and now in North Africa, New York City and Naples. The original Madrid church, which has had to move several times as it outgrew its premises, now meets in an auditorium capable of seating 1200, and has an average Sunday congregation of 450—the largest Protestant church in Madrid.

Today a team of 80 national and expatriate workers conducts all aspects of the operation under the leadership of Elliott, Lindsay, two missionary pastors and nine national pastors who have at one time been addicts.

Approximately 15% of those who have come into the centres have been completely rehabilitated. Some have stayed with Betel, fired with the vision to free others still gripped by the same bondages that once held them. Many have found their way back into normal society again.

'You are so naïve!'

What is the secret of Betel's success? Elliott has a good friend who was the national president of a worldwide Christian businessmen's organisation. Astounded by Betel's managerial methods he said to Elliott, 'I know the secret of Betel. It is because you are so naïve that you do not even realise that this thing can't work.' Elliott's reply was: 'The truth is we take drug addicts, prostitutes, people who have never held down a decent job, some of them almost illiterate, and we make them administrators and pastors. We teach them vocational skills and we entrust tens of thousands of dollars into their hands. This year almost three million dollars went through the centres and I did not handle it. They handled it; I only supervise its use. And it works. It is pure grace. It is pure mystery.'

The dark cloud

No description of Betel would be complete without including a reference to that dark death-bringing cloud which hangs over all its work—the AIDS epidemic. Because of wanton living in pre-conversion days many of those set free from drugs are HIV positive (possibly 75%). Funerals are part and parcel of Betel life. But there is an incredibly bright side: those who are its victims, realising that their time on earth is limited, exhibit an abandonment to Christ, an awareness of the eternal, that puts normal Christians to shame.

When interviewed on a Dutch television programme, Elliott said this: 'We began the work on the streets, among the outcasts, the untouchables, the drug addicts, the prostitutes and the alcoholics. These people came to us looking for help. They received Christ and God changed them, but almost all of them have the AIDS virus. I imagine three-quarters of them have it. Rather than making us a sad church, it has done two positive things:

'First it has turned these people away from the world. They do not belong to it any more. They live on the edge of eternity. Every one of them knows that they have the sentence of death inside, and rather than fall into deep depression, they have begun to walk in holiness and the fear of the Lord. Every moment of life is to be valued.

'Secondly, because of their background as addicts and prostitutes, they have turned their back on normal society; they have said 'no' to average living. That makes it easy for us to place the heavy demands of true discipleship upon them because they have already left everything behind. There is nothing to give up except their sadness, their sorrows, their criminal judgments, and their vices.'

The succeeding pages reveal a common denominator in all the conversions—the impact of the love shown by the Betel staff. But firm handling is also needed. Here are some of the rules:

1. New entrants must cease using illegal drugs.
2. All legal drugs will be supervised and administered by the staff.

3. Smoking and the use of all tobacco products are prohibited.

4. All individuals will participate in the full schedule of the community's activities, i.e. meals, work, meetings, etc.

5. Each person will accept at all times a personal monitor who will accompany him/her during the early months of rehabilitation.

6. A new entrant will spend the first fifteen days on centre premises under supervision, and after that may leave only when authorised by staff, and in the company of a monitor. (Note: Anyone can terminate his/her stay at any time. The motto is 'easy entrance, easy exit'. No pressure is applied.)

7. Couples, whether married or not married, will be temporarily separated on entering the centre until the staff feels it is right for them to live together. A couple not legally married will not be permitted to maintain sexual relationships within the community.

From the Levante to the Levant

What about Betel's future? The possibilities are breathtaking. Noel Ellard, a converted Irish alcoholic, has a vision to see Betel established in Ireland. Lutz Damerow of Germany was converted when he visited a Betel community in Spain. When he finishes seminary training he plans to help Betel start in Germany. Kent and Mary Alice Martin, American WEC missionaries who have been with Betel since 1991 and are members of the Madrid pastoral team, are preparing for Betel to start in England. Marseilles or Nice are in the Betel leadership's vision for a commencement in France. Betel has also received invitations from churches to open centres in Mexico and Ukraine.

During a recent investigative trip to Italy the Lord met the leaders as they travelled by van and gave them a vision:

FROM THE LEVANTE TO THE LEVANT. This would mean the ministry advancing from its bridgehead on the Spanish Mediterranean coast (the Levante) to the coasts of Syria and Israel (the Levant) via Southern Europe and North Africa. Work has already started in the Spanish enclave of Ceuta, a seaport bounded on three sides by Morocco, and in Melilla, another Spanish enclave 200 miles east along the coast.

What a vision! What a work of God! Readers will be awestruck by the mighty, sovereign grace of God as it reaches into the filth and degradation of human life to save and transform ruined men and women into saintly servants of the Lord.

A word of explanation. The writing of this book has been a team effort. In 1993 Stewart and Marie Dinnen visited Spain and recorded the 'raw material'. Elliott Tepper gave unstintingly of his time explaining the work of Betel, recounting the story of its beginnings and giving a conducted tour of most of the centres. He and Kent Martin (formerly a journalist) acted as advisers and translators. In Valencia, Lindsay and Myk McKenzie acted in similar capacities.

Back in Tasmania, Diane Griffiths transcribed the recorded stories which the Dinnens then edited in collaboration with Elliott, Kent, and the McKenzies. (Thank God for FAX machines!)

Last, but not least, the book could never have been written without the honest heart-revelations of those who shared the deep but gracious dealings of God in their lives.

Stewart Dinnen
Launceston
Tasmania
March, 1994

HOW DID THIS NIGHTMARE BEGIN?
The story of Raúl and Jenny Casto

'Give me the money, or I'll kill you!' I yelled at the shopkeeper, holding the point of a knife to his neck. Terrified, his wife cried, 'No, no! Don't kill him. Take the money.'

As I fled down the street with enough cash for a few 'fixes' I was shocked at what I had done. I asked myself, 'Raúl Casto, why on earth have you done such a despicable thing? How did this nightmare begin?' But I was desperate for a fix, and after taking it I had no more qualms.

Raúl is from a working class family of seven children in San Blas, Madrid. When he was thirteen he decided to quit school and at fifteen began to work, but never stayed at anything for any length of time, although he learned a bit about plumbing.

While still a teenager, he began to smoke 'joints'. As usual, his taste for marijuana soon gave way to hashish. Hashish gave way to amphetamines, amphetamines to LSD—and the chase began, one 'high' after another up the one-way ladder to addiction.

In a few years' time his body felt like a walking laboratory, testing the combined effects of multiple drugs and alcohol three times a day. It was when he was on leave from the military (between the ages of eighteen and twenty) that he finally reached the top rung and began sniffing cocaine and heroin—two plagues to which his suburb of San Blas was succumbing. Heroin gave him such a beautiful, relaxed sensation that when he felt like vomiting the first few times, even the nausea felt good.

Raúl continues:

13

After military service I went to Africa for ten weeks to work as a plumber. I saw this as an opportunity to throw off drugs, but I found more in Equatorial Guinea than I did in Madrid. This was a turbulent period for me; I did not relate well to the other workers and was often in fights. The authorities almost sent me home.

When I came back all my friends were into mainlining with heroin and I just followed them. I also moved into selling drugs—that was an easy way of earning money. But soon I was completely hooked myself, and spent all the money taking stiffer and stiffer doses.

My need was so desperate that I resorted to a life of crime in order to obtain money. I burgled during the day, taking things out of stores, and I stole at night, robbing people on the street, sometimes threatening them with a gun or knife.

We discovered that the Metro people moved the money from the ticket booths at the same time each night; so we would go just before that and rob the takings for the day. I often did supermarkets, threatening the cashier with a knife or a toy pistol, my face covered by a mask.

I never thought to go to a government clinic for help. On the one hand there weren't many and on the other they didn't seem to be able to help people very much.

I managed to get a job in a laboratory. I worked there for nine months and was then due for a holiday. I met Elliott Tepper on the streets of San Blas who persuaded me to go to RETO centre in Santander for help. I thought I would give this a try but had no intention of staying longer than the length of my vacation. There I found people who had exchanged the needle, knife and pistol for the Bible. But I rejected their ideas and came home after fifteen days.

Raúl tells about the impact of a Nicky Cruz tape:

A cured addict called Angel invited me to his house to listen to a tape. It was by Nicky Cruz from New York. I was astonished at the change that came over his life when he accepted Christ. This made a deep impression on me.

But things grew steadily worse. My family and my girl-friend of five years rejected me. There I was, ruined, without mental or physical strength; I even thought about taking my life. That period of about five months was the most wretched time I ever experienced.

The turning point

In January 1986 I was on the street in San Blas, utterly dejected, wiped out and going through withdrawal, for I had no money. Lindsay McKenzie, a missionary from Australia, came by as he often did and started talking to me. He persuaded me to go to his flat at 131 Carretera de Vicálvaro: and that was the turning point of my life. Lindsay had never taken in anyone like me before so it was a bit strange for both of us.

I went through 'cold turkey' withdrawal and had no feeling, no purpose, no desire to do anything. It wasn't painless by any means. Anyway, Lindsay cared for me, took an interest in me, cooked meals and generally tried to involve me in whatever he was doing.

On the sixth day I said to him, 'Lindsay, I want God to change my life.' He guided me in a prayer of repentance and then led me through to faith in Jesus. That night I couldn't sleep. This wasn't from withdrawal, but rather because I felt as if there was a cable connecting me to God. My heart and mind were saying, 'God! God! God!' I had a completely new sense of peace and love. The insatiable desire for heroin disappeared and I began to see everything differently.

I began to search for answers to all that had happened to me. I could not comprehend the new situation. I had never read anything but sports magazines, but now I had this compulsive desire to read the Bible and to spend time in prayer. I discovered the truths about Jesus' sacrifice for our sins, and his resurrection. I wanted to know him more and more. I started attending all the Christian meetings I could, and had a great urge to tell people about the change in my life. We went out to witness in the streets day by day.

I was actually with Lindsay for four months before anyone else joined us. I spent a lot of time with him and Elliott and they answered many of my questions. We did Bible study every morning for three hours and were often up till 4 am discussing spiritual truths.

As time went on and other fellows started arriving, Lindsay gave me more and more responsibility because he had many other things to attend to. Eventually eight other men came to live in the flat with Lindsay and me.

Two months after his conversion Raúl went to a Christian conference in Guadalajara. Between 400 and 500 people were there, and God spoke to him. 'I don't want only to CURE you, I want to USE you!' He kept this to himself.

Then God opened a remarkable door of opportunity. John Blake, the director of the Billy Graham 'Decision' office in Spain, needed volunteer workers for the International Conference of Evangelists in Amsterdam. He contacted Elliott who recommended Raúl.

God enlarged his vision in Amsterdam of the church universal and planted a burden for missions in his heart. It was a tremendous experience for him. One day he was travelling back from Talavera with Myk and Lindsay. Raúl said, 'I don't really know much about love. I don't think anyone has ever really loved me.' At that, Myk, who was sitting behind leaned over and put her arms around him. 'Well, Raúl, I love you.' He felt as if it were the arms of the

Lord around him at that moment. Raúl continues:

What greatly encouraged me was that others trusted me. Lindsay would give me money to go and buy food and other items. And when he went off to marry Myk I was given total responsibility for the other fellows.

We leave Raúl at this point in order to introduce Jenny. She was one of six children and her mother was a Christian who went to church every week, so Jenny knew all about the Lord. But she didn't have a personal relationship with him even though she taught Sunday School for years at an Anglican church in Hamilton, New Zealand.

Jenny shares her testimony:

When I was fourteen I went through confirmation. I really wanted to take that step. When the Bishop laid his hands on my head, in my heart I was saying what he was saying and I really believe I received the Lord then. About that time I had an experience in my bedroom one night. I saw this great light and knew it was the Lord's presence. I cried out, 'I love you, Lord.'

I took over being superintendent of the Sunday School from my mother and continued in that until I was sixteen. However, I was going to school with other girls who weren't Christians and I decided to go with them into the things of the world. I stopped going to church, and teaching Sunday School and started going to parties, drinking. I moved out from home and continued living like that for seven years, one of these in Australia.

Back in New Zealand I was influenced by a homosexual fellow and tried heroin, but I vomited a lot and couldn't eat anything so I knew I could not go on with that. But I smoked hashish and took LSD and cocaine. Finally I was thoroughly

17

sick of it all. 'There's nothing to life' I thought, and I asked myself, 'When have I ever been happy?' Then I remembered. It was when I was at school and going to church. In fact they called me 'Happy' at school. So a new resolve came, 'I'm going to see if I can find God'.

I moved to another city and started going to different churches. I found a bit of peace but I didn't really find God. I spoke to a minister in an Anglican church and told him that I'd once taught Sunday School. I also told him where I worked.

Miracle after miracle

One Sunday I was working in the shop. It was pouring with rain, so there were no clients. I was sitting out the back crying my eyes out saying, 'God, I'm so depressed. I haven't found you; I've got no friends.' In the end I said, 'God, if you're there, do something' and the next client that came in was this Anglican minister with a big smile on his face. He said, 'I haven't come to buy anything—I've just come to see you.' He went on to ask if I'd like to teach Sunday School.

I realised then that this was the answer to my prayer, so I asked the Lord to forgive me for the mess I had made, to come afresh into my life and change me totally. I began reading the new Bible my mother had given me two months earlier and it came alive.

I used to swear like a trooper. The next day it had totally gone. Miracle after miracle! It was so exciting. I knew I had to leave where I was living, so I prayed for a cheap house by the sea where I could live alone. God gave me a little place by myself for $10 a week. If I stood on the bench, I could see the sea. He answered my prayers and gave me a new job; everything just fell into place.

Jenny began to attend an Assembly of God church in Hamilton. The Lord spoke to her about Bible College and she felt guided to the Orama Fellowship on Great Barrier Island. She had a year there and entered wholeheartedly into college life. The fellowship also had a rehabilitation programme, so she mixed with addicts and that gave her experience that was to be valuable later.

After college the Lord kept speaking to her about missionary service in Yemen, so she decided to visit the Auckland headquarters of the only mission working there —WEC International. Allan Shadbolt, the Director, felt that she had a call to missions and invited her to attend the candidate orientation course.

A few weeks after starting, the staff called her in to say that they didn't feel Yemen was the place and that she should seek the Lord afresh. When she did that, he clearly spoke to her about Spain. When she shared this they all felt that it was right. She was accepted for service for 1985.

Jenny describes the start of her life in Spain:

I arrived in Spain during March, 1986 and went to live with Myk Hall who was sharing a flat in San Blas with two other girls.

Raúl — and romance

One day there was a soccer match between the men of the San Blas church and another WEC-related church in Talavera. The teams were made up of Spanish Christians and a few missionaries. Raúl was playing for the San Blas team, and at that time he had been a Christian for three months.

After the game we all went over to the church and someone introduced us. 'Jenny, have you met Raúl? This is Raúl Casto.' I said to myself, 'I know this name. I know this

19

person.' Yet we had never met! Something inside me gave me the sense that I knew him.

My background is totally different to Raúl's. I have Christian parents and the help of a loving home church. Two different people—my mother, and Alison Shadbolt, the wife of the New Zealand leader of WEC—had told me that I would meet my future husband in Spain.

After our initial meeting Raúl and I quite naturally met up with each other in the course of church life. One night he walked home with me after the meeting and as he went off he said, 'Thank you for letting me walk you home.' I couldn't sleep all night, thinking 'Why should he thank me? Is he God's man for me?' The next day I said to the Lord, 'If this is your choice for me please confirm it.'

I felt that even if he were for me he was such a new Christian I would simply have to wait until he reached some degree of maturity. But as time went on I knew I really was in love with him.

Now Raúl continues the story of the friendship:

One morning in April, 1988 I woke up and it seemed as if one word was written over my heart—JENNY. I knew the Lord was confirming in my spirit that I was to marry her. I kept this to myself for a week, but it was like having a bomb ticking away inside and I had to talk to someone, so I sought out Elliott and said, 'I'm in love with Jenny and I believe it is God's will we should marry.' Elliott fixed his eyes on the ceiling for a few minutes (as he often does) and then said, 'Well, just keep it in your heart for a while.' He turned to leave the room and then looked back at me. 'Mary and I have been praying for this for a long time.'

Jenny gives the details of how the matter was settled:

20

I came up to Madrid about a month after that happened. I was working in Torrijos and I hadn't seen Raúl for six months. I went to the San Blas church for a service. Raúl wasn't there so I felt fairly relaxed. Elliott said to me, 'Jenny, you have to speak to Mary; come and have a meal with us.' Sitting in their living room Elliott asked me if I had anyone in my heart as a possible life partner. I said, 'Yes.' He said, 'Who is it?' I didn't really want to tell him but just then he walked out of the room and I said to Mary, 'I feel the Lord is speaking to me about Raúl.' Elliott came back in and when I told him he said, 'Well, Raúl has told me that the Lord is speaking to him about marrying you.'

I was so shocked I couldn't believe it. I sat there with Mary, and Elliott went off to call Raúl who was staying in Alicante at the time. Elliott said, 'The woman you've been thinking of marrying thinks the same way about you.' He had such a surprise he dropped his plate of soup.

We arranged a date and I came up from Torrijos. We went for a walk. He said, 'I know you don't speak Spanish well yet, so you don't have to say much! Just "yes" or "no". Will you marry me?' I said, 'Yes.' We were married four months later.

Devastating news

About the time we were engaged, I asked Raúl if he had antibodies of AIDS. He said 'No.' He had been tested six months before coming into the centre and the result had proved negative. I asked him because my mother had asked me. It was important to her.

So we were married and when I became pregnant four months later the doctor said it would be a good thing for us to have blood tests seeing Raúl had been a drug addict. I and the baby tested negative but Raúl showed up positive, which meant he had antibodies. We just went into shock. We went

21

to see Lindsay and Myk McKenzie, and Raúl just cried and cried.

We had to face up to the situation. Of course the simple facts were that, at that time, he was well; we were called to serve the Lord; and we were called to each other, so we went ahead *by faith*. We lived like that for two years. During that time Raúl had two trips to Equatorial Guinea.

We were then sent to Barcelona to commence a new work. It was very successful and grew to the point where we needed to rent accommodation for over thirty young men.

We went on holiday but Raúl developed high temperatures and diarrhoea. When we returned we went to hospital and they kept him in, giving him test after test to try to find out the source of the problem. He became so ill it seemed to me that he could die.

We really cried to the Lord during this time and he encouraged us with confirmations of his purpose for our lives. After six weeks they found that he had tuberculosis of the stomach and the intestine. It had punctured his stomach wall and spread to other parts. He was in a great deal of pain.

Faith did not mean ignoring this. It meant facing the facts of Raúl's condition, crying out to the Lord, getting a word from him, and then going on in the strength of that word, knowing that what God said we were going to believe. God showed us that the doctors weren't going to operate even though they told us that it would be necessary. But we knew God was saying he was going to cure it with antibiotics, and in the end, when it turned out to be TB, antibiotics was the treatment they used. By the time he came out of hospital his defences had gone from being very high to very low—the result of the delay in correctly diagnosing his condition.

We kept expecting that we would go permanently to Equatorial Guinea and so returned to Madrid, leaving the work that was developing well in Barcelona. Raúl was very weak and I was now pregnant for the second time. The baby arrived and we had tests revealing that both of us were HIV positive. This result really threw me into a spin. I had thought that even though Raúl had antibodies the Lord would protect me. I cried, 'Lord, why do I have to have this?' But then he showed me that he was not going to seal me off from the problems and the hassles of the world; that I was going to pass through them the same as anybody else but that he was with me in them.

Ever since that question and answer I've known that it has been for my best. From the very first moment I knew that I was infected, God has just filled me with a new feeling of compassion towards others similarly afflicted and a new love towards the people in the church. I am able to say, 'It's worth it.' The people know that I'm where they are at, and that really has helped me.

In the past I had felt I wasn't particularly useful, that I did not have a really vital ministry, but now, since having antibodies, I feel God is able to love through me and to show his mercy through me in a new way.

Raúl feels now that it is not possible for them to go to Equatorial Guinea—it would be like signing a death warrant, so they have accepted that. The latest word about the baby's condition is that the tests are now negative. A high percentage of children born HIV positive lose this condition within the first two years.

What of the future for Raúl, Jenny and the family?

Jenny continues:

A pastoral role

Elliott came to talk to us about our future. He said, 'The church in San Blas is growing. We have not been able to

23

concentrate on the church the way we would like because of our responsibilities in the centres, and the church needs to be pastored. We've tried to do it but there is so much to do among the addicts. We want you to preach more, visit the people, and begin to take a pastoral role.'

I was excited because that's all I've ever wanted—to do counselling and work with women in a church situation. Also we know that Raúl has pastoral gifts and that this ministry would really suit him.

Raúl concludes:

We don't want to give the impression that we are living in victory all the time; there are days when we are really under the weight of the whole thing. What God has done through this—and I don't think he could have done it any other way—is that he has broken something inside me. Also, it has enabled us to relate personally with the people we are dealing with so that the others can't say, 'You don't have this, you can't understand our problems.' We are on the same level.

We are ministering to those who come for advice as well as to the people who are part of the church but are not connected with the rehabilitation work. And I am constantly on the telephone counselling younger workers who were under my leadership in the early days.

Having AIDS makes us realise there is no time to waste; we want to live intensely for the Lord.

THE GROWTH OF
BETEL

1

THE BACKGROUND TO BETEL
by Elliott Tepper

On our arrival in Spain in July 1983 we were naturally drawn to the university people. We thought we could relate to them best. God had given us an elite group in Mexico[1] and we thought he would do the same thing in Spain. I enjoyed interacting with students, talking, arguing, and trying to win them, but God just did not seem to be working in that mode.

The students showed no interest in the gospel or the things of God. They were content; they had everything. They had lots of money, fine health and good prospects so they rejected our message.

New vision, new frustration
One day the field leader, Billy Glover, and I were talking and praying in my office and the Lord seemed to impress on our hearts the idea of starting a new pioneer advance. We took it to the team and they agreed that we should start a new outreach in the Madrid neighbourhoods of Concepción and San Blas and in the agricultural town of Tarancón. Since we live in San Blas we became the spearhead of that group. Billy, some of the other WECers, and I would go on the streets with the sketchboard, passing out tracts and talking to people.

We decided to start a home meeting on Friday nights. This was the beginning (by faith) of a new church. For the first three months nobody came! Just Mary, Billy and I—

---

1. See chapter 5 for details of their time in Mexico.

that was all. Finally a few people started to show some interest in the gospel and would take the tracts. To our chagrin they all turned out to be drug addicts. No normal person showed any interest, not the working class people, not the middle class, only the drug addicts, and usually they had some ulterior motive. They wanted money or wanted to manipulate us, asking us to pay their electricity bill, or buy milk for their babies. We did not know how to help them because we had not worked with drug addicts before. We knew of existing Christian rehabilitation centres like Teen Challenge in Burgos, the REMAR centres in the south and north of the country and of one local centre in Madrid.

I remember the second addict we took to Teen Challenge. We were delivering food that had been given by the churches, so we took this drug addict along. I do not remember his name, although I do remember the look on his face and the state of his hands. It was as if he personified death, decay and deception. We had to drive through snow almost half a metre deep. We stopped at a restaurant and this man shot up in the bathroom. Back then we did not have the presence of mind or, for that matter, the authority to search addicts' belongings for drugs and syringes. I remember seeing his syringe lying on the floor of that filthy bathroom; you wouldn't ever want to use the facilities, let alone take out a syringe in such a place. These guys were deceiving us all the time, but we were on the lower slope of the learning curve.

New dimension, new density
We dropped him off and I remember being impressed by the spiritual life of Teen Challenge. Many of the churches in Spain lacked vital spiritual life, yet here I found a group of about twenty ex-criminals, covered with tattoos, who were full of life, full of God, and keen to go on. I felt as if I was

back in Mexico. I sensed the same spiritual hunger, the same common ground. That was the beginning of my desire to work in a community drug centre.

One fellow we took to Burgos came back to Madrid faster than we did, even though we were driving a car and he was hitchhiking. I don't know how he did it. You can put a drug addict on the moon and he'll get back without a spaceship!

About this time Lindsay McKenzie, a new Australian WECer, started to attend our meetings. A little later God also spoke to him about having ministry experience with addicts, at the REMAR Centre in Vitoria. As he had already completed formal language study, the Mission agreed he should go there, while we continued in San Blas.

I remember REMAR's first farm in Vitoria. They had only one building. Miguel Diez, the leader, had thirty people living in it with no electricity, no plumbing and one toilet that didn't work properly. The conditions were primitive, but I found hunger and life among the REMAR drug addicts. These people were hungry for God. They had slipped out of the materialistic first world, out of their Spanish pride, out of Europe into a sort of sub-culture. They were really broken and needy, and knew it. When I came back I was very enthusiastic. I saw by faith that this kind of work was going to prosper marvellously. Miguel had also started a church alongside the drug centre. People were starting to attend and they were also starting businesses to finance the centre. Money was coming in and the work was just about ready to take off.

Myk Hall had arrived in Spain from Australia in August 1982 and had spent time in two WEC-related churches. Though she appreciated her experiences with them, she did not feel she had found her ministry niche. Lindsay encouraged her to get some exposure to REMAR's work among drug addicts in the north of Spain. This proved to be a providential suggestion. For once Myk had taken that step she was further prepared for the leap into the work that was opening up in San Blas. As a missionary nurse she felt drawn to the physical and spiritual needs of the people. Her REMAR experience of actually living with prostitutes and addicts rounded out her professional training as a nurse.

New call, new commission

I said to Mary as we were standing in the kitchen doorway, 'If we're willing to work with drug addicts, prostitutes and alcoholics, God is going to give us a church, a great church, and he is going to give it to us fast.'

As soon as I said that the Holy Spirit fell on both of us. We had a divine call to start the work and we have never looked back. We had a word from God. It wasn't our idea. God called us, and gave us a Pentecost experience. When that happens, then you can do anything; you can walk through a wall; you can walk over a mountain. It's supernatural; it's sovereign, and has nothing to do with men.

Once we both had taken that same inward step of faith committing ourselves to this ministry, love began to spring up in our hearts for these people and their families.

Parents started bringing their sons and daughters who were on drugs to our home meetings. We would serve refreshments and discuss how we could help them. They were not interested in the gospel—they wanted help for their kids, but they kept coming regularly.

The first parent that gave the impression of being saved was Maruja. We sent her son up to Vitoria and she made her own personal commitment to Christ. She was sincere and grateful, but I doubt if she was really saved. Then one day she was diagnosed as having cancer in her uterus and had to go into hospital for an operation.

Since we had no church yet, we took Maruja to the old WEC Pueblo Nuevo church, anointed her with oil and prayed for her on Sunday. When she went to the hospital on Monday for the operation they found she had no cancer. She had experienced a miraculous healing and could not help but testify to her friends. Soon lots of them started coming and the meetings began to grow.

Finally we started meeting some valuable people and these early converts are our pastors today: Raúl, Pino, Tito, Manuel, Miguel and others. Raúl, Manolo, Angel and Tito had been the inner circle of gang leaders in San Blas so their conversions had a dramatic impact on the district. They were the 'tough guys' and people noticed the radical change in their personalities and behaviour.

When Lindsay came back from his six month stay at REMAR we used to walk the streets of San Blas. We would talk to people and generally they respected us, but there were always some who were out to deceive us.

One time two men tried to rob me brandishing a small knife. I probably could have beaten them up or run away—they were so drugged and sickly. We were witnessing as a group in the plaza in front of the Torre del Campo bar. It's amazing, but I was stupid enough to move away from our group and found myself alone with my two would-be assailants around the corner of the building. A drunk off-duty policeman just happened to pass by and rescued me. They both went on later to make a commitment to Christ.

Their names were Victor and Buenadicha. Buenadicha was another 'tough guy' and a deceiver. He was a wheeler-dealer and a big thief. He had rotten teeth and a very bad attitude. He developed endocarditis, which is a very typical disease for drug addicts—an infection of the heart. If it reaches a certain stage and one's general health is poor, it is incurable. If you have good health, you can treat it with antibiotics. But these people have very low resistance due to AIDS, bad diet and their undisciplined, chaotic lifestyle. For them endocarditis can be fatal.

Miracles in the body, hardness in the soul
Buenadicha was in and out of Betel, but could never seem to get his heart and attitude right with God. As his health deteriorated on the street he was forced to enter the hospital suffering from very high fevers and an accelerated heart rate. The doctors thought he was going to die. They gave him up. I remember visiting him, sharing the Lord with him, and then praying for him. I laid my hands on him and asked for healing in Jesus' name. God healed him instantly. He came out of the hospital and along with his wife, children and much of his extended family began to fellowship with us. He seemed to do well for a while but then he backslid.

When you help someone, the family often starts to take an interest in the gospel. His brother-in-law also attended some of our meetings. He had mental problems and begged us to let him enter the centre, so we were quite happy to offer him a place. I remember feeling that God through us would be able to help him. He had taken a lot of LSD and had lost his emotional equilibrium. He was fearful and paranoid. Doctors, psychiatrists and medication had not helped.

The week he was going to enter Betel, the other side of his family convinced him that we were a sect and frightened him away. A few days afterwards he jumped off the fourth floor of a building and committed suicide. His death was a tragedy, but I take some comfort in knowing that he had heard the gospel and had a strong desire to live with God's people. Eternity will reveal the secrets of the heart.

There were other outstanding miracles of healing that did much to encourage the faith of the church and make an impact on unbelievers, but which did not result in a lasting commitment to Christ on the part of the person healed.

For instance, Lolo was working on the roof of the Mejorada farm when he suddenly fell through the corrugated asbestos sheets some ten feet to the cement floor. We had no telephone at the farm so he lay paralysed for two hours before we could get him to a hospital. He was X-rayed and it was discovered that he had broken two of the lower bones in his back. The whole church prayed on Sunday and he was healed instantly in his hospital bed. Lolo told me that the power of God flowed through his body like fire. He got up and walked out of the hospital. He passed by the church once to say thank you, but went right out into the street and shot up. We never saw him in church again. We heard that he had become a big 'camello' (pusher), selling drugs and earning lots of money. He died recently of AIDS, far from God.

We have found—both in the early days and later—that even though God works a miracle of healing, as in Buenadicha's case and in Lolo's, it does not necessarily follow that the person will become a Christian. But often, God will use such miracles to touch others and somehow extend his Kingdom.

It's all been done before
Betel is not a unique expression of Christian drug rehabilitation or community living. There are many historical precedents. Recently I came across the biography of Pastor Hsi, a Chinese Christian of the 19th century who was converted from his opium addiction by China Inland Mission missionaries. He went on to start a network of Christian rehabilitation centres, churches and community businesses. I was amazed at the similarity of vision and method between his work and Betel's, over a century later.

A close friend of ours, an American Pastor named Jack Growblewski, spent about two weeks with us visiting our centres. Towards the end of our time together we were standing on the roof patio of our Ceuta centre in North Africa, looking out across the straits of Gibraltar to Europe. We could observe the men below going about their duties; some were climbing into vehicles to be transported to the different jobs in the city.

He said, 'You know Betel is really much like the medieval Franciscans.' Jack is quite a scholarly fellow and I was pleased that he had made the comparison. I thought to myself, perhaps we are like them: holy, other-worldly, humble, a true spiritual community. Next he added, 'Yes, you're just like them—another bunch of guys who don't know their right hand from their left, trying to eke out a living together while they serve God.' That took the wind out of my sails. But he was right. There is nothing special about our vision, or us!

Full house demands a fresh start
In the beginning, for almost two years we simply referred our contacts to the existing centres and worked with their parents in Madrid. All the centres in the beginning were small. Inevitably we reached a point where the RETO and REMAR centres were full. I believe we were referring more addicts to them than any other missionaries. They told us they couldn't help us any more. Miguel Diez said, 'There are no more beds, and in any case, we don't want to see any more addicts from Madrid. They are the worst in the country!' It is true. The Madrid junkies are the hardest people. They are aggressive and unteachable. If there are eight new men in a dorm, the one from Madrid will demand to be the leader as his right. And often the others let him.

We had to do something. Lindsay had an apartment

above the church and so we took the first addicts there. Together we carried the burdens of each of those first addicts. We laughed, we cried, and we prayed as we saw God doing what he wanted to do in Betel. It was God who was doing it, we were being obedient. It was an exciting time. Raúl was the very first and that was the start of Betel.

Leaps of faith

Later on, as the Betel work started to grow, we had to find a large property, a farm for our growing resident community of addicts, and that required a lot of money. We didn't have any; we were all struggling just to survive in an expensive country. We were believing God, like everyone else, for our monthly support.

We looked at a farm in Barajas but the owner did not trust us because we were foreigners and because we were working with drug addicts. He would only consider letting us have it if we paid a year's rent in advance and of course that was way beyond us.

We sought the Lord and he sent a $3,000 gift from a man in the United States, a friend of WEC staff member Elwin Palmer. He didn't even know me. He simply heard, through Elwin Palmer, that there was an American missionary working with drug addicts in Madrid. Back then—nine years ago—that was a lot of money, so with that gift we paid the one year's rent in advance and moved in.

The Valencia property was another chapter in our faith ventures. Lindsay and Myk McKenzie came back from home leave in Australia and were ready for a fresh challenge. We talked together about Valencia and he decided to go and look around. We found a property but needed $5,000 to clinch the contract. But we did not have that kind of money so we took it to the Lord. We waited on him and told him we were trusting him. He worked for us and sent a gift

35

of $5,000 from friends in Kansas City who knew us and loved us. They had never sent such a large donation before, and they knew nothing about our need.

This enabled us to rent buildings that were sufficient for a church, a furniture store, offices and a residence for girls. I think it is important to see the principle here—we committed ourselves, by faith, to starting in Valencia before we had the money. We made our declaration, we stood in naked faith, we claimed what we needed, and then God provided.

Not only have we seen the Lord's supply for housing and expenses, we have proved his sufficiency when we have had bad accidents. Some of these have been very costly. We had a situation where one of our men took out a vehicle which was not insured. This is strictly against our rules. Well, he had an accident and we were presented with a repair bill for the other car amounting to 110,000 pesetas (then about $1,100). We were simply not in a position to pay this, and I remember we were standing in front of the office discussing it when one of the leaders of the Full Gospel Businessmen's Fellowship walked up to me and presented me with a cheque for 110,000 pesetas—the exact cost of the repairs. God showed us that he was watching over us, even in our mistakes.

Why this waste?

Naturally, most of our people are undisciplined; their minds are often affected by the drugs and they don't act wisely. They don't look after the cars; they forget to put oil or water in them; they overheat them; they have accidents; they burn out our generators; they run the batteries down; they destroy transmissions. They are so wasteful. One day I asked, 'Lord, why all this waste?' and he said, 'That's exactly what Judas asked. This is the cost that goes with trying to help people. The cost of valuable souls. This is what it costs to

36

build the kingdom of God with this kind of people, and it's not wasteful to me.'

We outgrew the first church building in Vicálvaro where the WEC offices are now. We had about 120 coming to church on Sunday. The meeting hall was only about 40-50 square metres. We had people packed in like sardines, standing in the entrance and way out into the street, so we had to move, but we had no money. We were paying about $300 a month towards the mortgage payment on this locale which was a multi-purpose centre.

Faith relishes the impossible

We had to find a new place. I searched and searched. I went through all the neighbourhood of San Blas, all through the Madrid city area. We thought for a long time that God would give us the Cinema Argentina which holds about 1000 people. The owners wanted $4,000,000, which was un-thinkable.

Then one day I was driving along a route I seldom take and I saw this old white building with a large patio. The door was open so I stopped and looked in. It was like being in Mexico again. There was a courtyard, a pavilion. It was a two-storey building. Then I saw the owner, Mr Julio Gomez, standing in the inner doorway. It turned out that the property had been unused for about fourteen years and there were even trees growing in the cracks in the middle of the patio. It had been a dance hall with a stage. It had a large 180 square metre room without columns in it and a high ceiling. It had a second storey with three large rooms, large public bathrooms needed for a dance hall and some space for offices. Outside it had a pavilion and a floor for summer dancing.

So I talked to Julio and asked him if we could rent it and he said 'No,' he was not interested. I kept after him and wouldn't let him go. Finally after about two weeks of pestering him and trying to meet every stringent condition that he demanded, he said he would rent it to us. I asked if we could buy it outright, but he refused. He said it was worth a fortune and he would not consider selling it.

It is an old building, once a stable, built in the last century and is not set straight according to the street line. At one end it is about two or three yards in from the building line and at the other it crossed over onto the sidewalk. In Spain all buildings have to be a certain distance from the main thoroughfare, and the reason he had not rented it for fourteen years was because he would have had to take down the offending section of wall and rebuild it.

According to the zoning laws it was only suitable for residential or non-commercial use, but our church fell into that very category! Those two factors—the cater-corner construction and the zoning—allowed us to take it. We had to pay about $3,250 a month rent—almost eleven times what we were paying on our old building. We had no reserves, no savings, and were just making the $300 a month needed for the place where we were.

In order to take it we would need to have the value of three months' rent—two months as a deposit with the government's property chamber, and one month in advance to the owners. That meant about $9,000 up front; and then we needed thousands of dollars to renovate the building. It needed to be re-wired; it needed new plumbing, and half the roof had to be replaced—a lot to do, and the total cost, about $20,000.

So we made an offer; he accepted it, and then we had to come up with the money. We prayed, we went to the Lord, and then told the church, and from that young congregation —many of the people just recently converted and most of them very poor, such as cleaning women, factory workers, drug addicts and many on unemployment—we came up with the $20,000! We were able to pay the initial $9,000 to complete the contract and then, over the next two or three months, do everything needed to put the building in order and to pay the architect. God provided, but again we had to take a step of faith before we had anything. And God met us. The workers did some heart searching and came up with several large gifts; everyone helped and gave sacrificially.

We were there for about two or three years, and during that time the congregation grew to over 300. Once again we were filling the building to capacity and spilling out into the patio. We simply had to have another building. Even to find one was a hard thing because in Madrid the lots are very small—people build upwards to save horizontal space. The cost of a warehouse or commercial site would be astronomical.

The pinnacle — so far

One day I drove past a building that had been used as a book factory and a printing warehouse. I had asked about it because I knew that it had a floor area that could seat 1,200 people and it had a basement which ran the whole length of the main floor. The first time I had enquired the owners had asked for $4,000,000 or $25,000 per month rent.

This time I saw the door open so went to have another look. I was so impressed I asked other team members to inspect it, so six of us went—Paul Anderson, Armando, Raúl and Jenny Casto and Mary and I. We walked through it and all said 'This is the perfect place for us'. We went through every part of the basement and main floor claiming it for the Lord. Then I made an offer. I offered $7,000 a month instead of $25,000; I explained that we were a Christian charity working with drug addicts and that we just didn't have that kind of money but we'd like the building.

The man's name was Mr Silvano, a very wealthy builder. He said, 'I'd like to help you but that's an absurd offer. Give us a better offer. Maybe we'll come down and help you but let's be realistic.'

So we waited; we didn't want to jump right at it. We prayed more, claimed the building and I offered him $9,000. He said, 'I'm sorry, I've talked to all the directors of the corporation, (a big real estate company) and we can't let it go for $9,000 a month. There's no way. We'll let it go for $15,000 a month.'

I told him we couldn't pay that, and we left it like that and waited and prayed more. Then I came back with another offer and I said, 'We will give you $11,500 a month.' It was our final offer and he took it, and by doing so had cut the original price by more than half.

But that was only the beginning. We had to come up with three months' rent in advance—$34,500 and we did not have any money. We had just the minimum of reserves to keep the drug centres functioning—$3,000 to $4,000 in our savings account. Neither did the church have that kind of money. So we had to go before the Lord, then challenge the church members. We started a long-term faith promise system for monthly donations. Everyone would pray about the amount they would commit themselves to give on a regular basis. Then we had one special offering for the building and that raised $10,000. All the Betel centres in Madrid decided to run a calendar campaign, going out on Saturday afternoons. Finally we put all these resources together and found we had $20,000.

We had one more hurdle. The owners were business-men, and because we were a charity that worked with drug addicts, they were very suspicious and said, 'Either pay us the whole year's rent in advance or come up with a guaran-tor who has assets to cover that amount.'

We were in the process of buying several properties at that time but did not have the titles to any except a small house in Almería. However our good friends in the Christian Literature Crusade, a sister organisation to WEC, came to our rescue and after much time-consuming legal and financial negotiations we were given the keys. We had paid a large deposit but the owners would not allow us to occupy the building or begin renovations until the guarantor's document was finally signed. Much time had been lost and instead of having a two month grace period for the changeover we had only two weeks before the first monthly rent payments were due.

We had to vacate the former church building at Calle Raza, move everything to the new centre and turn the old property into a used furniture and appliance store in order to start earning money to cover the cost of the remaining seven months' lease we still had on it. At the same time we needed to make the new centre useable.

The printing factory had a centimetre of ink, glue and grease on the floor and we had to use caustic soda, grinding machines and scrubbing machines to lift it. We re-wired many of the circuits; we ripped out the old lighting system in the ceiling which was three storeys high; we renewed the plumbing and built bathrooms; we raised walls to separate the nursery and kitchen from the main seating area; we put in offices on the mezzanine floor. We had to put a new sewerage system in. We ran sewer pipes half a metre in diameter through the whole length of the building and then out into the street. We installed a new sprinkler system, as a fire precaution—all this in only two weeks!

Sometimes we had up to 100 workers swarming like bees in every part of the building. As the opening day on Sunday, January 3rd drew near, we worked frantically to clean the floor and paint the walls. Two of the multiple bathrooms, for men and women, were made functional and electricity was laid on temporarily. We did not finish till eleven o'clock on the Saturday night—less than twelve hours before the opening service. God was with us and we did it.

By the month of May, five months later, we had the building almost fully refurbished on the ground floor and on the mezzanine floor.

The basement is still virtually untouched. Recently, the Billy Graham Association asked for the use of the buildings as part of their Campaign in Europe where Billy Graham preached by satellite to almost all the European nations. They chose three sites for the showing of the Billy Graham relay in the Madrid area, and Betel was one of them. It was the largest site in the country. We had approximately 1,000 people seated in the auditorium for the preliminary concert and then had 700-800 people each day of the campaign.

Our building is the largest Christian evangelical auditorium in all of Spain and also serves as our international administrative office. Our Sunday morning meeting is the largest evangelical meeting in Madrid. To God be the glory.

In November, 1994 we rented the other half of the book factory for our largest 'Rastro' (thrift store), public admitting offices, dining hall, furniture repair shops and central food dispensary. This gives us an additional 22,500 square feet of space at our Headquarters.

2

TRIUMPHS & TRAGEDIES
IN THE EARLY DAYS

God's purposes involve people—called people, committed people, people to whom he gives spiritual gifts in line with his calling and purpose.

God knew that a married couple with four boys would never be able to house and care for drug addicts, so he prepared a young single man 13,000 miles away in Melbourne, Australia for this initial demanding task. Lindsay McKenzie was in retail management before attending WEC's training school in Tasmania. Learning how to live communally, to communicate cross-culturally, and to submit to discipline were all factors that helped prepare him for the biggest challenge of his young life that awaited him in Spain.

Arriving in Madrid during August, 1983 he was quickly immersed in the new worker's primary tasks—language study and cultural adjustment, but it was a great relief to have Friday afternoons away from the grind and to link up with Elliott and Mary Tepper in their efforts to reach the young people of San Blas.

Elliott had developed links with the REMAR rehabilitation centre at Vitoria run by Miguel Diez. On a couple of occasions Lindsay had been able to accompany Elliott when he took addicts there for help. The Lord started to lay on his heart a concern for these needy outcasts of society.

In accordance with mission policy Lindsay had to have a placement with a Spanish church in order to have more experience with a national pastor, but with the increasing

*burden for these 'marginados' (marginal people) he felt
strongly drawn to working under Miguel Diez at REMAR.*

*This was confirmed when the field leader, Billy Glover
said that the Lord had shown him the same thing.*

Now we will let Lindsay pick up the story:

With the WEC team's blessing I went to Vitoria and
admitted myself to the centre like anyone else, except that
I wasn't an addict!

I thought I had learned all I needed to know about
communal living at WEC's training school in Australia, but
at REMAR there was a *total* absence of privacy. Even going
to the toilet was not private—people wandered in and out
constantly. There were no such things as personal possessions. Everything belonged to everybody. There was no
electricity and during the winter the water would freeze in
the pipes.

But it was a great experience—one of the best times of
my life. I learned another aspect of sacrifice there. I had
tremendous insights into the Spanish mentality and to the
drug sub-culture.

I had never smoked or touched drugs so during these
seven months I was plunged into a totally new way of
thinking.

*Back in Madrid it was agreed that Lindsay should work with
the Teppers in San Blas. On Friday afternoons the team
would gather and intercede for San Blas and the huge
addiction problem that surrounded them. Not yet having a
centre of their own, addicts who were willing to go were
taken to existing centres elsewhere, but the team reached
the point of despair when none of these they had transported
at their own expense would stay, let alone become Christians.*

But they held on in vital intercession seeking God for a breakthrough. And it came! Lindsay continues:

Both RETO and REMAR sent back word that the young people we brought from San Blas were the hardest they had ever encountered. Although humanly they were not at all inclined to take any more, Ray Pollnow of RETO thoughtfully said, 'Send me some more; I would like to find out what the spirit is behind their tough attitude.'

Ray is a very discerning missionary and after a time he sent back word. 'There are two demons governing San Blas; one is called "Lying"and the other "Deceit".'

The breakthrough

We had a witness in our spirits that he was right so we began to direct our prayers, exercising our authority over these two spirits. We sensed we were getting through to God and that something was happening in the heavenlies even though we did not see any visible results.

But within a month—towards the end of '84—the spiritual climate started to change and people began to stick with the programmes and to come to Christ.

On 1st January, 1985, we sent a fellow nicknamed Hippi (his true name is Miguel) to RETO. He stayed, and subsequently became a leader there. A month or so later his sister, Begonia, went and later became a Christian. Their mother who was attending our church in San Blas became one of the pillars of the fellowship.

Then a girl called Toni, realising that these people were being changed, went there for help, and shortly after that her brother Santos joined her. Their mother was converted in our meetings.

So we knew the resistance had been broken. The behaviour of Begonia before and after our spiritual 'breakthrough'

45

is an interesting case. Before that, she had gone to REMAR and stayed only two days.

I remember seeing her on the street after that, painted up and back at work as a prostitute. She looked at me and sneered, 'I'm O.K. now; I don't need God,' but she was soon into drugs again. After the breakthrough she returned and really met the Lord. This time, when she returned she said, 'God has saved me, and I really know him now.'

In April '85 Miguel Diez asked if the team would like to have one of his new workers with them in Madrid for a few months, just to help and give some input. Elliott, Mary and Lindsay thought it would be good so a converted addict, Ramon Aguilera, joined them in July and was a great asset. Myk at this time was at REMAR in Vitoria.

Meanwhile, with increasing contacts and a new responsiveness to the gospel it became more and more obvious that the team needed to develop its own facilities for the care of addicts.

By this time the mission had purchased a 'locale' (ground floor area in a high rise building, designed for use as a retail store or workshop). Part of this was used as an administrative centre, but the large front room was used as a church meeting place. It was ideally located on the edge of the suburb of San Blas.

It was obvious that if the team was going to do anything to help these needy men, they needed to live in San Blas and close to the 'church' at 131 Carretera de Vicálvaro. For three months they prayed and believed that God would give space within that complex, and then Lindsay found a flat on the eighth floor.

Ramón came to live with Lindsay, and for six months he was part of the evangelistic outreach, participating in our intercessory times when they prayed through to victory over the forces of darkness. His life and testimony were a tremendous help as a Spanish 'role model' and he was greatly missed when he returned to REMAR.

Lindsay, without even realising it, took the first step towards a new rehabilitation programme. He describes what happened:

Raúl Casto was a gang leader and a pusher—a well known colourful figure in the drug world. His nickname was 'El Tocho', the fat one, because he's quite well built. He told us that he had a court case coming up in a couple of weeks and he just needed somewhere to stay till then so I said, 'Come to my flat.' I had no thoughts of commencing a centre—I just wanted to help him out.

But during that time he came to the Lord and asked if he could stay on! We all sensed that God was doing something and that Raúl was part of his plan.

What do you do with an addict when he's living with you? Well, he just did whatever I and the team did. If we went on street evangelism he did it too. He wasn't even saved when he started, but there he was, giving out tracts!

Encore please

After three months Raúl said, 'What you have done for me I would like to do for someone else.'

So we discussed the possibility of taking in a second person, and along came Javi. His mother had been attending the church and came to the Lord. Her life was totally changed and she became a vital member of the fellowship. But Javi was a dead loss. He seemed to have nine lives. He would put seven spoonfuls of sugar in a cup of coffee, and he would chew the dregs just to get more caffeine into his system. He was even run over by a Metro train after falling on the tracks; he had been hit by cars; he had been shot and

47

knifed and is still alive. But after six weeks with us he left.

After that came Paco. He had been to RETO but proved so difficult they would not have him back. His mother, father, brother and he all came to church one day. A meeting was going on, but they fought at the door because his brother didn't want to come in. Eventually in walked Paco, thin as a rail, with all but one tooth rotted away—the most pathetic figure you would ever see. (Today he is a wealthy business man; he owns his own home and a number of vehicles; he and his wife have been fully restored.)

We decided to take Paco in; he became a Christian and we discipled him up to the point where he was participating in the local 'Decision' evangelistic campaigns.

Two others came to us at the same time—José and Manolo. José had been in prison seventeen times in twenty five years. Violent, and somewhat mentally retarded he was difficult to handle. He was super-sensitive and paranoid.

Manolo had just come out of prison and he wanted to be in our care. He had failed so many times and deceived us, we were just exhausted at the thought of having him, but he arrived complete with a big dagger and a huge kit-bag of clothes. He dumped them in the doorway of the church and said he wasn't leaving. This alarmed the shopkeeper nearby who phoned our apartment saying he was scared because this man was a well-known addict.

That pressured us into action. I slept with him one night in the church just to see what he did and the next day he came up to the flat.

So there we were—four drug addicts and myself at that stage. But Raúl was a big help. He was a born leader. We did all sorts of things with these fellows to keep them busy. We had them cleaning the flat, painting it and painting the church downstairs. They didn't have any jobs; they didn't have any money, so we had to make jobs for them. We went to the local wholesale market to ask for food because by that stage finance was a problem. How were we to feed all these fellows? They all ate like horses after coming off drugs!

Then in December, just as the weather was becoming colder, two others arrived at the church on the same day— Vigi and Luis; Vigi had been a jeweller. They were both so dirty it was embarrassing. How were we to take them up to the apartment without the neighbours noticing? They were already nervous with so many addicts in the building. In these apartment blocks, you cannot hide; you cannot be private. Everyone knew what was happening and didn't like it much. They started talking about us and against us. So, we made the fellows have a shower, a shave and a haircut down in the church before we took them up to the flat.

Vigi was the most unbelieving guy I ever met. He was materialistic and full of unbelief. He couldn't conceive of anything that wasn't material. Luis on the other hand was a man who didn't have any character—no personality. He just drifted through life. Very passive.

Friction in the flat — rumblings in the block
Can you imagine the atmosphere in that small three-bed-room flat with six or seven of us there? Paco and Raúl were the only two who were converted. They were quite happy to accept the situation. We didn't know where the others stood spiritually. There were all kinds of rebellion, jealous-ies, fights and shouting and many times Elliott had to come over to be referee! I was beyond being objective! Every one of these Spaniards was a Franco. All chiefs and no Indians!

We carried on with our evangelistic activities. These fellows would hand out tracts whether they believed in what they were doing or not. We had learned from REMAR how to do street theatre and we taught them. One drama was called *The Chains of Man*. It illustrated the different stages

49

the drug addict went through, from smoking to drinking to taking drugs. It is a very pithy powerful drama. People would cry watching us. We could hold 300-500 people in a park and it was more effective than months of planning and dozens of church meetings or a big campaign in a stadium. Many people would listen to these drug addicts for long periods.

At this stage we had so many men in this small flat that the neighbours had a meeting with a view to throwing us out, but the Lord intervened and it didn't happen. From then on we knew we had to leave because we were just causing too much distress. People were afraid to ride the elevator.

There were two aspects to all this. While some were afraid of us, the shopkeepers were happy because, since we had been there, they had not had any hold-ups. The breadshop lady said, 'I feel safe when you men are around, I don't know why, I just feel safe. Before, I felt scared but now I've met some of them I realise they are real people and they are getting fat, and looking a lot better—like real people.'

The Spanish leader of 'The Decision' ministry, José Luis Briones, had a sister who lived in the same building. She was travelling on the Metro to San Blas one day and two of the drug addicts tried to rob her. She said, 'Hold on a second, I'll give you something.' She took a tract out of her purse and they said, 'Oh, are you with the Betel church?' She said she was, so they said, 'Then we won't rob you!' and let her go. And this did not just happen once. So many were converted that the crime rate started to go down!

The last one to join us in the flat was Luis Pino. He is now the leader in the Madrid centre, and also the National Administrator. His mind was so burnt-out he could not add three numbers together. Now he controls millions of dollars and he's brilliant—he has a touch of genius but he was never a natural leader. We were frustrated with Luis because he was, as they say in Spain, an octopus—just flowing with the current. He couldn't make any decisions and always wanted to please others. Now he has obvious gifts of leadership and he's not scared to confront people.

The story of these early contacts would not be complete without mentioning three more whom the team tried to help. One of these had the street name of Dupi although his real name was Javier. Lindsay describes him as being 'overbearing, proud, handsome, athletic and super-emotional.' He was persuaded to go to RETO but he lasted only a couple of weeks. Back in San Blas he stayed in touch with the team and even attended some Bible studies, but he drifted off again.

Then one day—about a year after he had left the RETO centre—the team picked up word among the San Blas residents that the police were looking for Dupi because he'd stabbed one of the local pushers and killed him. Dupi had asked the dealer to give him some heroin on credit and he refused because he'd failed him in the past. So Dupi said if he didn't give it to him he'd stab him. The pusher said, 'You haven't got enough guts to do that.' Dupi said, 'Haven't I?' With that he thrust at him to just scare him, but stabbed him in the heart. So Dupi was now a murderer, and wanted by the police. He was on police bulletins; his name was printed in the press but no-one knew where he was.

Lindsay describes the next part of the saga:

On the wrong side of the law

Two days later I had a phone call from the Pollnows of RETO in Santander. Dupi was with them! He wanted to return to Madrid to give himself up but first he wanted prayer with us and then he would go to the authorities. He would be arriving by train next morning.

Elliott and Mary were on holiday so I decided to contact

51

Myk, my fiancée; we agreed we would go to the station for the 7 am arrival.

We were never so embarrassed. He rolled off the train drunk. We rushed him to the car so that no one would see him, but where were we to take him?

Then we thought of the Tepper's flat—it had a private entrance. So we took him there, gave him something to eat and let him wear off his drunken stupor.

Then we thought, 'What have we done? We're harbouring a criminal! We have committed a serious offence.' And we could hear helicopters overhead—probably looking for him!

When he came to his senses we said, 'Come on, Dupi, let's go to the police.' He said, 'No. They will only beat me up. I want to go and give myself to a judge.' It was true— some police were known to do that. They would extract their vengeance on him before handing him over. He wanted to say goodbye to his family because he knew he would be locked up for years. What were we to do?

We moved him surreptitiously to the WEC church premises. We couldn't ring up his parents because their phone was tapped, so I made my way by an indirect route to his parents' place. I told them that he was down at the church and that he was wanting to say goodbye to them before he went to the authorities. So they said they'd come. I asked them to do it in an indirect way and not to let the police follow them because we didn't want to become involved too much.

They took ages to come. Myk and I were wondering if we'd done the wrong thing. Maybe we shouldn't have agreed to this! The mission could be involved. Anyway the mother and sister came and said a very emotional goodbye. We said, 'Come on, hop in the car and we'll take you to the court house.' He said, 'No, I've decided I'm not going!' We told him if he didn't get in we would wash our hands of him and he could take the consequences. So finally he was persuaded. We hid him in the back of the car and drove him to the Central Court House.

He was given a twelve year sentence. Of that he spent four years in prison and he's now walking free. He's proud of the crime he committed, in fact he uses it. He says, 'Be careful with me; I've killed someone before. I won't think twice about doing it again.'

Myk returned from REMAR in October 1985. On the same basis as Ramón had been sent to us, REMAR also lent us Dori Pájaro for four months—a sweet young ex-addict. Together Myk and Dori led worship in the public meetings, sang and did drama in the parks, then started a girls' Bible study in Myk's flat.

Myk recalls:

We took in a tall skinny girl called Anna as she went through withdrawal; then we sent her to RETO. Next was Isabel and she went to REMAR after withdrawal. Never have I seen such degradation and squalor as when I went to help her pack her few possessions at the tin shack she had shared with her boyfriend.

When Mari Carmen asked if she could come off drugs at our house I checked with my flatmates Jenny Scantlebury and Anne Stoddard. They were quite willing. She came through the worst of the withdrawal and was at the stage of simply needing encouragement, massages and frequent fluids. I left her making lunch while I went out. On return, I was greeted by Jenny with the news that Mari had disappeared. We found her on the steps of her old hang-out, smoking a longed-for cigarette. I burst into tears and begged her to return. A few days later she did turn up, announcing,

'I've decided to come back.' I had hoped that she would be the first of a women's Drug Rehabilitation Center at my flat, but we had to send her to RETO when her husband Manolo turned up demanding entry to the men's center.

The Lord had other plans and we had great joy when the first Betel Women's Center started in a flat in Vicálvaro, ten minutes away, just after Lindsay and I were married. Estrella was our first women's leader.

Two more early dramatic incidents will live forever in the memory of the Betel pioneers. Elliott describes them:

Demon cast out

One day, after doing open-air evangelism using a sketch board, we brought a group of young people to our apartment, gave refreshments and then had a gospel meeting. While I was speaking one of them tried to take over. He stopped me and said, 'Look at me!' He glared at me with a terrible demonic look on his face. I couldn't ignore it, so I said, 'I bind you, Satan, in the name of Jesus and I cast you out in the name of Jesus.'

At that he spun around in the chair as if someone had wound a rope round him and pulled it, like a child pulling a string on a spinning top. He opened his mouth wider than you would think possible and began to scream. The demon left him and he was set free. Once he had come to his senses I asked him the name of the demon and he said it was a spirit of incest—he confessed to sexual relations with his sister. It was just incredible. But he left and never returned.

While we have seen many dramatic deliverances from demonic power with a lasting change in character, that was one instance in which we have seen the Lord deliver someone, yet they haven't gone on to real spiritual life or growth.

But others were different: Dameon, for example. He went berserk at our Mari Blanca chicken farm and tried to kill the people at the farm with a knife and club—one moment he would act like a killer, the next like a lamb. The men brought him to my office while he was acting like a lamb. We prayed for him, taking dominion over the evil spirits in him. He shot up out of his chair, went rigid like a plank of wood and leaned forward at a 45° angle into us spitting and screaming and then was suddenly set free.

Today, two years later, he is one of our missionaries and principal leaders of Betel in Italy.

3

ADVANCE TO ALMERIA

The Betel team is constantly on the look-out for God's leading to new developments. Sometimes he does it through giving a vision, sometimes through an invitation from an outside party, sometimes by a word from the Lord himself.

The story of Almeria, which Elliott Tepper now recounts, is typical of many such advances.

We were first made to think about a move to the south when a pastor in a small town called Barbate approached us. He had a church building which he was willing for Betel to use as a centre. At the same time a local government social department there had a property which it wanted used as a rehabilitation centre. So we went to see it but for a number of reasons felt restrained about moving in. The town was quite remote from other population centres, and there were already other good groups working in that general area.

All this led us to think about the south, and it was agreed that Tito, who is now leader of the New York work, and I, should spend a week exploring the southern coastline, seeking to be sensitive to the Spirit's leading.

We started in Algeciras. I really liked it but REMAR was established there. We went on to Málaga, but Daniel Del Vecchio's group was established there, so we kept going east along the coast until we reached Almería.

It was here that we sensed a real peace from the Lord. We were able to rent a small house which became our initial base. Downtown, we also rented a vacant truck depot. It wasn't large and it was full of grease and grime. But the location was excellent so we knew that with a new floor and a clean-up it would be usable.

The leader is the key

Back in Madrid we started to think about the need for a leader in Almería, and we quickly sensed that Tito was the man. He is an apostolic figure, now capable of living away from the community, where he had been for three and a half years. One can identify personalities who have faith, vision, and a vital relationship with the Lord. Leaders have to be strong spiritually, emotionally and mentally, but I would not say physically, because many of our leaders are very sick people. They do need to have initiative, be self-starters, and have some commercial sense.

So we decided to send Tito. He made some suggestions regarding other team members. We wanted at least two strong, faithful men who could be trusted with money and who were stable morally. Then we looked for a few who needed a change, and could benefit from a fresh challenge. Lastly we looked for some who were a few months old in the Lord and would stick with the programme.

The team eventually consisted of Tito with his wife Isabel, and five other men. A van and a car were supplied from Madrid resources.

When we start a new centre nothing can be accomplished until our publicity goes out. But the leaflets can't be printed until we have a telephone, and that, in Spain, is no easy matter. However once we are connected, we print leaflets that say something like this: 'We are a non-profit Christian rehabilitation center offering a free resident program to all who wish to enter. Our supervised work teams paint, clean, do masonry, remodelling, farm work, loading, unloading, distribution of advertising, etc. We also receive donations of used clothing, furniture, appliances and other

used objects in good condition for our second hand store.'
Out of tens of thousands of leaflets distributed we may have
100 calls, and that gives us a start.

Ruin for a residence

From our initial base Leo and Tito started exploring,
looking for a suitable residence for those who would join us.
They found a large abandoned house outside the city, but it
had no windows, doors or plumbing; it had been gutted. It
was a place where junkies would shoot up; where prostitutes would go with their clients. It was a real sore in society.
They decided to take possession, clean it up and occupy it.
As far as they knew there was no owner and it was not
registered at any government office.

But after three months a German gentleman who lived
in Luxembourg arrived on the scene, claiming to be the
owner! He did not want to kick us out, however, but he
wanted us to recognise his ownership. He was quite generous and entered into a contract with us whereby we could
have the use of it for $60 a year.

They found another abandoned building on top of a hill,
300 metres above the sea. It had been a restaurant, but it had
been gutted. The roof and the floors were all broken up, and
it had no plumbing.

We are not thieves! We do not mean to steal property if
it belongs to someone, but many of these places have been
totally abandoned; no title deeds exist; there is no registra-
tion in the government property office, and the original
owners are not likely to ever come back.

There was a time in Spain when whole housing developments were built without planning permission. Things
have tightened up now, but this building was part of such a
project. Probably the owners went bankrupt.

The team talked to the council officials but they had no

idea who owned it. So they obtained their 'blessing' to occupy it and actually gave them a written document to that effect. The police know we are there and are very happy about our using it because it means that it will be kept out of the hands of junkies and prostitutes.

Our goal is to see a living church planted in the area among the addicts who become converts. Our hope is that they can then reproduce themselves spiritually in the area, survive economically by finding a commercial niche, and so have a strong foothold in the community. All this may take three or four years, and initially, if we do not find many addicts locally, we import them from other centres, so that there is a viable community to which new people can come. After two and a half years, Almería had 72 people, 50 men, 15 women and seven children of whom a few are from Almería itself. Some of these have families who have started to attend our meetings.

We are gradually winning the confidence of the local people. We have to keep working at relationships, so we send the men who have a good presentation to businesses, factories, markets and warehouses. Our motives are three-fold: to obtain work, receive food and materials, and to make Betel's programme known.

We established the principle of 'testifying' to business people in Madrid. Perhaps nothing comes from an initial contact, but gradually firms loosen up and start giving. Sometimes they give junk and we have to take it straight to the dump, but at least we are providing a free service for them by removing unwanted goods and gaining their good will. In the long run we are usually successful, receiving much that is really valuable. For instance we have a relation-ship with a soap factory which means that we never have to buy soap, shampoo, etc. We pick up out-of-date supplies of soft drinks, biscuits, bread, dented canned goods, etc.

Frozen food companies call us in from time to time and we fill our freezers.

Usually our income equals our expenditure. We make money from selling second-hand furniture, from painting and decorating, from distributing our calendars and so on. If we have any reserves these are usually used up buying vehicles, or financing new advances elsewhere. Our people live humbly in dormitories and much of the food they eat is given from the wholesale markets which we visit at the end of the day.

Almería has been very, very fruitful in many ways, and this has been due, largely, to Tito's strong leadership style. He is positively aggressive in his faith. It was through his vision that a new outreach started at Ejido, 40 kilometres along the coast, where we have a men's residence and a store. Almería has financed the whole Ejido project and the team is also responsible for a new advance even further down the coast into Málaga, providing the first leadership team, vehicles and rental property.

Since he had proved the Lord in such a clear way in Almería, we felt that Tito should become the leader of a new advance in New York City, which began in 1992. At the end of its second year the New York work included over 20 people—10 of whom are American addicts—and four properties: a three-family pastoral residence (purchased by Betel) in Queens, a men's residence with 36 beds in a converted curtain factory in Brooklyn, an office and second hand store in Jackson Heights, and a large home across the street from the Queens' residence which is being re-modelled for a second men's residence and Tito's family.

4

THE VISION EXPANDS

Early in 1991 in the first 'Cumbre' (bi-monthly leadership conference) of the year, Elliott challenged the Betel team to consider Ceuta as a possible new center in North Africa and a springboard for advance along the northern coast and for entry to the Moslem world. Spain retains two small enclaves on the African coast from its former colonial possessions: Ceuta and Melilla. Both cities are ports of about 70,000 inhabitants and are under Spanish sovereignty. They are 'safe' stepping stones for staging and entry into the ever more turbulent Moslem scene.

Not long afterwards, Ian Borham, an Australian WEC missionary, having just returned from an exploratory trip to Morocco with another missionary who was based in Ceuta, encouraged us to set up a center there because there was a desperate drug problem among the Muslims in that city.

In May 1991, Lindsay McKenzie was sick in bed with flu. He was suddenly awakened and heard God clearly speaking to his heart: 'Juan Capilla and Eddie Hoho will lead the Muslim work in Ceuta'.

Lindsay continues:

My immediate response was: 'Lord, if you are really speaking, then please confirm it by saying the same thing to Juan Capilla.' (He was then second-in-charge in Valencia.) That week Myk and I invited Juan to our place for a meal. As we chatted I asked him what his longterm plans were about Valencia. A little embarrassed, he replied that he did not see himself staying there because God had called him to the mission field. Asked 'Where?' he replied, 'Africa.' I said, 'Equatorial Guinea?' He replied, 'Well, no. God has called me to work amongst Arabs.' This had happened four months earlier, but he had kept it a secret. At that point I shared what the Lord had said to me, and the three of us sat there speechless, marvelling at God's ways.

So it was decided to send an exploratory team to Ceuta, a ninety minute ferry ride from Algeciras, across the straits of Gibraltar. A group of five leaders visited and felt an inner peace about establishing a work there. They had useful contacts but made no move regarding property.

In October of 1992 Elliott, Lindsay and three of the Spanish leaders made another trip and found a suitable flat on Calle Real in the Spanish section of the city. It was expensive, costing almost $900 a month. In the Moslem section of El Haidu they also found a small house, half of which was available for renting. It was in a poor area where the streets are very narrow. The team could see that drug-trafficking was going on there.

Elliott tells us the story:

We found that it was not easy to survive economically in Ceuta because wages for Moslem people were about $5.00 a day, whereas Spaniards received $5.00 an *hour*. The Moslems were doing many jobs for much less money than we were accustomed to charge. For instance, in Madrid we would paint a house for $800-1000, but in Ceuta the same work would bring only $200. So we had a hard time. It is isolated from the mainland and its commerce is limited to its freeport bazaar activity, tourist trade and contraband trafficking with Morocco.

There is a significant drug problem among both the Catholic and Moslem populations of Ceuta, but the concentration of addicts is light relative to the mainland. So we did not have many coming to us. Those who did were Moslems and they had tremendous cultural and religious barriers to overcome.

We tried to build up a community among them, but we really didn't understand their culture. Ceuta is not an ideal location for a drug center. We knew that, but our goal from the beginning was to establish a base for entrance of the gospel into the Muslim world.

Learning to work with Muslims was a long process. They deceived us continually; they were always smoking and breaking the rules. Some would come in and rob us outright, just take everything we had. One fellow who had been with us a couple of months, took everything moveable and left. Another who was with us almost a year seemed to do very well; he was very sincere and had an obvious relationship with the Lord; he was humble, meek, co-operative. One day he was shadowing a new arrival who was going to pick up his unemployment payment, and the two of them went off to a house of prostitution. So we lost them. They never came back.

Spanish addicts didn't stay long either, during this time. We lived in a difficult neighbourhood. Eight times we had the battery taken out of our van; we had things stolen from the house continually.

We had a psychotic Moslem fellow who came to our centre a number of times, causing great problems. He had a split personality and threatened us with a knife on a number of occasions. After he left, he dressed up in a suit, shirt and tie, took a clipboard with him and went round collecting money 'for Betel'. We told him to stop, but he wouldn't. When I was down on a visit, Juan the leader asked me to go with him to report this man to the police. Later we saw him and explained that we loved him but that he must stop this behaviour. His response was to take a knife, and puncture the tyres on all our vehicles.

It was a very difficult period while we lived in the house in El Haidu even though we had developed an excellent relationship with some of the neighbours. Across the street was a brothel and a few doors down was a group of drug pushers, so it was just too much of a temptation for the men. The rooms were very small and we had only one public room where they could relax. It was not an acceptable situation so we began to pray for another place.

The miracle castle

The total area of Ceuta is only twenty square kilometres and very few buildings are unoccupied, so hopes of finding accommodation were small. We prayed, 'Lord, give us a house; we need a big house with some space.' Then we remembered that there was a big house on the hill.

We had seen it the first time we arrived in Ceuta, on our first exploratory trip. We drove by it often. It was near the military zone on top of the mountain. We coveted it from that first visit, and on the second we actually walked through it and thought it would be a fantastic place. We said, 'Oh Lord, give us this house in your time.' One day it was brought to our attention that it was now available, and that the owner was open to selling it. When we contacted him he refused to rent it; all he wanted to do was sell it, and of course he wanted cash and we didn't have the necessary $90,000.

So for a number of months we just let it go. A little later Tito, our leader in Almería, paid Ceuta a visit, and when we were driving past the house we noticed it had been painted white and was occupied. Juan immediately visited the owner and said, 'Why did you rent it out?' He said, 'I haven't rented it. I'm just letting some friends use it for one month.' So Juan said, 'Will you rent it to us?' He said, 'Well, someone has offered me $90,000 for it and they're going to pay me $10,000 a month, but I won't sell it to them; I'll rent it to you.'

When we took it over there were no window panes in any of the windows; all the plumbing was ripped out; there was no electricity or water, and part of the ceiling had caved in. The brickwork of the chimney was broken, so when we lit a fire the smoke filtered through all the rooms. As the months became colder we put plastic on the windows and lived without glass. We didn't have any money because Ceuta wasn't an economically viable centre.

Bit by bit we've put it into shape. We have glass in the bottom floor windows; we have warm, dry dormitory rooms for everyone; we have an office, a dining room and a chimney functioning properly; we have put in our own power plant. The first one was stolen by the Moroccans who crossed over the mountain and took it during the night. (We are only a few hundred metres from the Moroccan border.) Now we have five watchdogs on the property. This is also a source of income because we are providing kennel accommodation for them and receive $50 per dog per month for feeding them and delivering them periodically to their watchdog assignments.

We see this house as a channel for ministry into the Moslem world, a place of preparation, a place of hospitality and a place of intercession. Our house is the highest in Ceuta; only the army has a few installations higher than ours.

Morocco is 200 yards south of us. Spain and Portugal are north of us. To the east we have the lands of the Mediterranean as far as Israel and Syria. We are ideally placed for reaching out in spiritual advance.

Our house has a basement, ground floor, second and third floors and then a tower with an open patio. We can sit and watch the ships entering and leaving the Mediterranean and we can pray for Africa and for the Moslem world.

Our fellows are studying Arabic each week with an American missionary and are also making regular trips across the border to visit people and learn the culture.

Linked to Algeciras

Because of economic factors we realised we needed a base on the other side of the straits to help sustain Ceuta, so we decided to start another centre with a furniture store in Algeciras. These two centres now operate as a single unit.

We expect Algeciras to become a source of supply for Ceuta both in terms of economic resources and of manpower. We trust there will be Spaniards who will come into the centre there, find the Lord, be delivered from drugs, start to grow spiritually and then transfer over to Ceuta. It costs only $30 for the round-trip ferry ride.

There was only one evangelical church in Ceuta; it consisted of three groups that decided to come together—Brethren, Pentecostals and a gypsy congregation. They all worked together and we often joined in with them, but bit by bit it became evident that God had given us our own congregation. Each week a number of Ceutans meet with the Betel church for regular worship services in our house on the hill.

Early in 1994 Elliott and John made an exploratory trip to Melilla, about 400 kilometres east along the African coast, and rented a small Moroccan style house for the first men's center.

Today Melilla has an office, Rastro store and a larger men's residence as Betel's second base in the Muslim world. Melilla's Muslims are largely Berbers and not Arabic speaking and represent another door into the Moslem heart.

66

5

THE LORD PREPARES HIS PEOPLE
The testimonies of Elliott and Mary Tepper

*Although God has raised up a magnificent team to carry
forward the work of Betel, it is abundantly obvious that
there would be no Betel at all without the vision, burden and
leadership of Elliott and Mary Tepper. Here is their story,
starting with Elliott recounting the dealings of God in his
early life.*

I have always been a dreamer—a visionary—and a thinker,
and yet I enjoyed the 'good life'—fun and daredevilry.
From my earliest years there have been these two sides to
my character. I could be superficial and frivolous. At
Lehigh University I was into parties, fraternities, fast
motorcycles, skateboards (even handstanding on them).
But at the same time I was searching for meaning and
reality.

I was not brought up in a Christian home. My father was
nominally Jewish and my mother a nominal Christian who
had converted to Judaism. They were good parents. They
were liberal, success-oriented Americans who transmitted
to me their quintessential American values: patriotism,
generosity, kindness, excellence, and the notion that hard
work and drive, when accompanied by fair play, would
always lead to success and happiness.

My father was president of an electronics firm in New
York and partner in two other businesses. A man of vision,
he tried to do the impossible, and I inherited that from him.
My mother was a very practical person who loved to

entertain. She made our home a mecca for gifted and interesting friends and acquaintances.

For a season all my family touched turned to gold; it seemed as if all we tried and tasted in life was good to our palates. Likewise, success also followed me like a shadow. Friends would joke and call me 'the all-American boy'. But sometime after my fourteenth birthday my world began to unravel.

It was in that year my parents were divorced. Then, over the next few years my father lost his fortune. My mother, sister and I carried on in our large home on Long Island until I graduated from high school. Perhaps to the world, my life was still 'etched in gold'—I was an Eagle Scout, president of my class, New York State wrestling champion, and recipient of a generous wrestling scholarship to Lehigh University. I went on to study Economics at Cambridge University in England, and from there to Harvard where I received my MBA.

Hound of heaven on the track
While at College I spent three summers in Alaska, working on the salmon boats. I can remember my Indian captain, a Christian, talking to me about Christ, but I was so full of my own knowledge and so eager to disprove, not so much the existence of God, but at least his moral claims, that I would argue circles round him as we lay in our bunks after the day's haul. Glen would point to the mountains and the sea and reply, 'There definitely is a God. Look around you.'

I travelled that summer with Homer's *Odyssey* and I identified with the hero, Odysseus. The book was like a Bible to me. I read it when resting under bridges, in the forests and under the docks. I lived in its words, in Homer's heart and Odysseus's exploits. I had a kind of faith in an ancient invisible world that at times seemed to transcend the reality of the world around me. I had faith before I had faith. I used to 'live' by faith before I knew what faith was. That kind of spirit was always in me.

My last year at Harvard, I joined a commune and took part in all night discussions about politics and philosophy. That was when I started taking hallucinogenic drugs, hash-ish and marijuana. After graduating, I worked as assistant to the treasurer at the Boston Museum of Fine Arts.

During this period others witnessed to me about the reality of Christ and the need for a personal relationship with him. One girl from our commune, a biologist, went to Israel, then came back and told us she had met Jesus Christ. We thought she was crazy. I was a Jew; I had no loyalty to, or faith in, Jesus Christ. I thought this girl was strange but I could not deny the positive change in her.

I was stopped one day on the Charles River bridge. This stranger, carrying a knapsack and a Bible, turned out to be a Harvard scientist. Out of the clear blue he said, 'You are lost. You're dwelling in unbelief on the dark side of the Cross.' A cold wind blew right through my soul. For the first time in my life I started to fear God. I had believed in him as a child, but I took him for granted. I did not realise he was a moral God who made moral demands on my life. I began to fear that if I died I would spend all eternity separated from his presence.

Then I met some Christian hippies—'Jesus people'—in a laundromat. They had the same message about God's love.

Through a plate glass window
After that, I can remember walking one day along the banks of the Charles River on top of snow that was as hard as ice. There on the edge of the frozen river God spoke audibly to me. He said, 'Give me your life.' He lifted me up in a vision

69

and opened the heavens, showing me a glimpse of eternity and the new Jerusalem. In an instant I knew that all that I was seeking was in God and in eternity. I do not know why, but I replied, 'Yes God, but not today—tomorrow. There are still things I want to do.' At that moment I was brought down from the heights of my revelation to the banks of the Charles River and a vision of the earth was opened up before me. I saw the mouth of hell, a great declining slope that descended deeper and deeper into hatred, cruelty, and finally into demonic perversions and horror, into that place of ultimate, eternal separation from the love of Christ.

The vision was so real that I cried out, terror-stricken, for mercy, thinking that I had lost salvation forever. Not understanding the simplicity of surrender, I began to walk through the streets of Boston crying out to God. Finally, in desperation, I threw myself through a storefront window where I was cut very badly by the glass. A police vehicle carried me to the hospital emergency room and I was left alone on the table for a few moments. I prayed the first sincere prayer of my life and then Jesus—not physically, but by his Spirit—entered the room, filling it with a brilliant heavenly blue light. He asked, 'What are you dying for? I want you to live and have many children.' He touched me and filled me with the Holy Spirit. I was born again. I came out of death and darkness like a cork popping out of water. The doctor came in and assured me that I was going to be all right. I was sewn up and eventually sent home.

People have asked me how much of this experience was drug induced and how much true prophetic revelation. Only God can sort that out. But I can say this. It was not an hallucination, and what was burned into my spirit has not dimmed in over twenty-two years.

God pulls back the curtain

Within a few months of my conversion I left my Cambridge commune, the Boston Museum of Fine Arts, and the whole 'counter culture' of Boston behind and returned to my mother's home in North Carolina.

I began to attend a small church called the Seagate Community Chapel in Wilmington. One evening a missionary named A. S. Worley came to speak. I can remember him talking about his ministry among the tribes of New Guinea and our responsibility to take the gospel to the uttermost parts of the earth. He described the time he had preached for four hours to a group of stone age tribesmen, and when he had finished another tribe came walking up to the church. He was told that they had walked three days to hear the gospel and was asked if he would please preach again. He could not say 'no' and preached for another four hours.

After hearing that message I was never the same. I believe it was at this time that God put the call to missions upon my heart.

Shortly after this, I enrolled in the Faith Training Centre, a missionary training institute in South Carolina where A. S. Worley was the president. My life was greatly enriched and my burden for missions deepened. However, it was not for any particular country, but for the whole unevangelised world.

A. S. Worley told me once, 'Elliott, I've got to tell you something. You have a brilliant mind, but there's one thing you lack.' I thought, 'What do I lack? I'm born again, I'm filled with the Holy Spirit; the gifts of the Spirit work in my life; what do I lack?' He said, 'You need a "John the Baptist" experience! You need to be decapitated! You need to live from your heart and not from your head!' So I've accepted that lesson. I see from the heart. I don't see the impossibilities.

After one semester I married and left the institute. My wife, Mary and I, naïvely felt that at any moment we would hear God's specific call and then he would launch us out into world missions. After a year of working, waiting and being faithful in a local church I was frustrated, so I decided to fast and seek the Lord's direction.

One day, while we were fasting, someone called us on the telephone and said, 'There is a minister speaking in town at a nearby church who has the gifts of the Spirit operating in his life. I think you ought to hear him.'

We arrived and entered the service. He and his family were singing. When they stopped he said to the congregation, 'Costa Rica, no ... Costa Deir. Is there anyone here who knows Costa Deir?' I was the only soul who knew this man and raised my hand. Then the minister said, 'I don't know what this means, but I believe he has a word of guidance for you.' The Holy Spirit came upon me in power and with great peace. I knew God was saying something, but what exactly it was, I did not know.

We went home and that night I wrote a letter to Costa Deir who was the foreign missionary secretary for the Elim Fellowship in Lima, New York. I simply recounted what had happened. He sent me a very short letter which said, 'This is God. You come here.'

We moved to Lima, New York, and entered Elim Bible Institute. Elim is a great crossroads of ministry and missionary activity.

During our two and a half years there our vision of the purposes of God was enlarged and our calling to missions deepened. We finished our missionary course without receiving a clear word of guidance and so returned to North Carolina where I served almost a year as an assistant pastor in the church.

One day a missionary from Mexico named Jack Knowles

came to speak in our church. Jack and I had been classmates at Faith Training Centre. While I had left to marry, attend Elim Bible Institute and enter the pastorate, Jack had taken his family directly to Mexico as independent faith missionaries and the Lord had mightily used him, first in a thriving church in Mexico City and then to evangelise dozens of villages in the mountains.

I can remember sitting with Jack in our kitchen. My heart burned within me as he told of the responsiveness of the people. He turned to me and said, 'How old are you?' I replied, 'Thirty-one.' Then he said, 'If you don't go to the mission field this year, you'll never go.' I was smitten. I felt as if a prophet was in our midst. In that moment the Lord sent the shaft of his arrow into my heart with a specific call to Mexico.

To understand our strong faith emphasis at Betel, you need to know something of our background in Mexico.

We felt we could now move out in faith to the mission field. But first we presented our plans to the senior pastor and the elders of the church, trusting that they would confirm our calling. The elders gave us their blessing, but to our chagrin the pastor did not. We were in a quandary because we believed in submission to spiritual authority. During that difficult time our call was tested, but the Lord upheld us and assured us that 'we ought to obey God rather than men' (Acts 5:29). We quietly and humbly left the church and made plans to head for Mexico without guaranteed support.

Living on the minimum in Mexico
The first years in Mexico were difficult. We were young. We had three children. Two of them were in diapers when we crossed the Mexican desert. We had diarrhoea, vomiting, no water, and very little money.

73

A missionary visa cannot be obtained in Mexico, so we were forced to take a three day drive out of the country to the Texas border every six months. That six days of driving, plus meals and accommodation, was an expensive proposition for poor missionaries, but it had to be done. Sometimes we went with hardly any money—just enough for gasoline.

I remember one time we stopped at a restaurant and couldn't buy enough for a full meal. Mary burst out crying and said, 'My father never treated me this badly.' I thought about this. God is our Father and yet we were really suffering. That was probably our lowest point in Mexico. Yet, even during those lean times we had success in ministry right from the very beginning. Even before we could speak Spanish, I began to preach through an interpreter and God raised up a work almost immediately. The Lord proved himself to us there. We learned to live on almost nothing; we learned to trust him; we often had nothing to eat in the house, but when we reached that point God always provided. Our children never went without milk in our four years in Mexico.

I remember once we were at rock-bottom and had absolutely no money. The food was finished; the rent was overdue; there was no gas in the car. We sat there in the living room, with our three little boys. Mary just sat there on the couch, crying. We prayed, 'Lord, you just *have* to help us, we can't go any farther.' I'd gone to the mailbox that day and there was no mail, no gifts, nothing; it was the end of the week, with the weekend coming up, and there would be no more mail. It was the end, and we were finished. Then all of a sudden, a letter was thrown right through our open window. A mailman came by and threw it in. Now, they don't deliver mail to your house in Mexico. It goes to a mailbox, and they don't deliver in the afternoon! We opened the letter and it contained a gift from a church in Pittsburgh. It had been lost in the mail for about six weeks. God showed us that he is a real God, a living God, and he provides. It was a big gift. It was $250—a large gift in those days.

God also provided me with a university position as an economics professor. Mary and I were offered scholarships to study Spanish. This gave me a respect, which was God's way of opening the door to the hearts of the people who would later form the 'Amistad Cristiana de Puebla' church, which today numbers 4,000 members.

In our last year I began to sense an urge in my spirit to move on. We had helped establish a new church in Cholula, Puebla, and in addition were experiencing a small revival among the university students. We had a group of about twenty meeting regularly in our home. The Lord had even touched some of the faculty with the gospel. There was no human reason to move on, yet the Holy Spirit was tugging at our hearts.

The call and the confirmations
One day while in Mexico City, Wayne Myers, a grand old missionary with more than forty years experience, mentioned the great need of the Spanish people—39,000,000 of them, and only about 40,000 evangelicals, making Spain one of the least evangelised nations in Western Europe. He said, 'Since Franco's death, Spain is wide open to missionaries, but the people's hearts remain closed to the gospel.' When I left his home that day, I had a weighty burden on my heart that would not go away.

Shortly after that encounter, Norman Grubb's biography of C. T. Studd fell into my hands. My spirit leapt as I poured over the pages. Here was a man and a mission that daringly, through faith, chose to walk in the heights of discipleship. I sensed in C. T. Studd's life the same notes I had heard at Faith Training Centre and Elim: faith, holiness, sacrifice, and fellowship. Perhaps the quality of heroic sacrifice appealed to me most. In any case, I felt impressed to write WEC a letter asking for an application. They sent me preliminary papers and invited me for an interview at the headquarters in Fort Washington, Pa.

That summer we made a trip to the States. On the way we stopped at Faith Training Centre and I asked for Brother Worley's counsel concerning our decision to apply to WEC. I can remember waiting for his response as he sat slowly rocking in his chair on the porch of the big house overlooking the school grounds. He said nothing for a few moments, then he carefully said, 'I've known many WEC missionaries. It is the best mission in America.' Then he paused and thought a little longer and said with conviction, 'No! They are the best missionaries in the world!' I had always valued Brother Worley's counsel and rejoiced to know that he felt we were on the right track.

Around this time Mary gave birth to Timothy, so we decided that I would go on to Fort Washington alone. I was interviewed by Duane Olson, the candidate secretary who said, 'We have examined your papers and, tentatively, we feel that Spain might be the best for you.'

After that, I headed for Pittsburgh where I was to spend a few days ministering at the Church of the Risen Saviour. I had decided to make a quick side trip to New Castle to visit Mrs Claudia Miller, a dear old saint who, in her 90's, still interceded daily for missionaries. She lived with her Bible open on her lap and prayed continually. I had said nothing to Mrs Miller about Spain or my intention to leave Mexico, or of my interview with WEC the day before. When she opened the door of her home we greeted one another. The first words to come out of her mouth were, 'Pray about going to Spain. I believe God wants you in Spain.' Then she handed me a picture of King Juan Carlos and invited me to lunch. If I had had any doubts before, they were gone. I knew I could say like Paul, 'But now having no more place in these parts ... I take my journey into Spain' (Rom. 15:23,24).

Now we turn to Mary and learn something of her experiences with Elliott.

'Smith Wigglesworth' arrives

During October 1972 Elliott and I met at a home Bible study in Wilmington, N.C., which was then my home town. Little did I realise then that he was the 'man of great faith, like Smith Wigglesworth' that I had been praying for. For the next few months we had short conversations when we saw each other at Christian meetings.

In February, 1973 Elliott went off to Faith Training Centre in South Carolina. We began to write to each other and at the end of March, he wrote and asked me to marry him. I wrote back and said 'yes'. We were both writing and receiving about five or six letters a week, and that is how we came to know each other. He finished his four month course in the middle of June and we were married two weeks later. It was definitely not a normal courtship, but we knew the Holy Spirit was guiding us.

It was very clear from Elliott's letters that he felt called to the mission field. In marrying him I knew that that was my destination also. My own personal call came during the first year of marriage. We were at our church where a guest speaker was sharing. At the end of the meeting he asked all those seeking the will of God to stand up. Elliott and I did so. The Holy Spirit spoke to me so clearly. He said, 'Go forth to teach and to love. Go forth in the power of my might. You must be willing to be put into prison.' For all the times I had heard his voice, I was amazed at the clarity and at the power with which he broke into my often cluttered mind.

We were called to Mexico in the fall of 1977. Elliott

heard the call and I followed. We made a three week trip to Oaxaca in January, with our three boys, David, Jonathan and Peter, aged three, 19 months and 5 months. In early June, 1978 we moved out of our apartment in North Carolina and headed with all our belongings to Mexico. We went out as independent missionaries and we had no support. But the Lord taught me that when there was no food in the house and the can of milk powder was almost empty *he* would provide.

I learned to trust God when Elliott would go on trips to evangelise, leaving me with a few dollars, no phone, and no transportation. Those days were not easy. Sometimes I walked the floor all night when the baby had a high fever.

We went back to North Carolina every summer for a visit; and in 1981, seven months pregnant, I made the six-day, 3,000 mile trip by car with Elliott and the boys. In July I gave birth to my youngest son, Timothy. In the months preceding this visit the Lord had begun speaking to Elliott about being part of a mission, and in particular, a mission called WEC International. Elliott met with the candidate secretary and it was arranged that we would take the candidates course starting September, 1982. We were accepted as new workers for Spain in January, 1983 and a few months later left for Madrid.

Of course, many of our first Spanish converts failed and we would take these setbacks personally. We would go overboard trying to bring back the fallen ones, but later, when our first leaders began to stand for God and the Betel communities and churches began to prosper and spread throughout Spain, we could say that it had all been worth it.

6

TRAGEDY STRIKES

The Teppers' son, Timothy, knew the Lord and he loved the Lord because he had been saved at a very early age. He also had a missionary call. When the other boys said they wanted to be archaeologists or soldiers or doctors or whatever, Timmy always said he wanted to be a missionary like his daddy. He had no doubt in his mind from the very first years of his life that he was going to be a missionary. He seemed to be, in a sense, the most spiritual of the boys. He wasn't a perfect little boy; he was mischievous with a 'high energy' personality, but he knew God.

Leaders of a work of God which is penetrating Satan's territory attract relentless counter-attacks on themselves and their family. Elliott takes up the story:

We think of Betel as one continual blessing after another, but we've also had lots of trials.

When we were home on furlough in 1991 in North Carolina, Mary was invited to the Presbyterian Women's Conference in Virginia. She felt that she shouldn't go, but finally went, all the time sensing intuitively that something was not right. She really did not want the boys and me to go off to Kitty Hawk, where we were going to spend two or three days at the beach for a men's holiday.

I wanted to do something special and I guess I pushed a little hard, which is my nature. We packed up and got ready. Timmy was not feeling too good; he didn't want to get out of bed, but I encouraged and coaxed him, and he was an obedient son.

David had just received his driver's licence the week before and was excited about being able to drive. I let him do so, probably wrongly, and put Timothy up in the passenger's seat in the front. I sat in the middle seat, and Jonathan and Peter sat in the back.

I was excited because I had a son who could now drive. I could sit and rest. We prayed before we started the journey; we committed our lives to the Lord, then I read the first four Psalms out loud and we sensed the presence of God in the car. We were full of joy, we were reading the word of God, praising God and it was such a happy time that I just burst out in praise and said, 'I thank God for four great sons.' I turned to the boys and said, 'Boys, you're going to be great. God has made you great, but just promise me (and I don't know why I said this) that you'll remember the one who made you great is God. Promise me that you'll always remember missions, that you'll remember where you've come from.' Then I said, 'Thank you, Lord, for my sons.'

They opened up the ice chest, took out some sandwiches and passed them around. That was an error on my part. I should not have allowed David to eat while he was driving; he was a young driver. I distracted him, I'm sure. Timmy didn't want to eat, he wanted to sleep and I remember adjusting his seat belt. He had his belt on and was using the upper portion of his belt as a pillow so I straightened it out so he could put his head on it, I gave him a kiss and said, 'Timmy, I love you,' and David reached over and rubbed his brother's arm and smiled at him.

Timothy's death
Within a few seconds we came to a curve and the car slipped off the edge of the shoulder. We went off the road and the van flipped over a number of times. No-one seemed to be hurt. It was a freak accident.

80

I hit my head on the roof and David had a cut from the window; most of the windows had burst open and glass was everywhere. But then I noticed Timmy wasn't in the front seat. I leaped out the side window and I looked back and there he was, lying on his stomach but looking up. He was at the side of the car and looked at me with perfect recognition, just a peace in his face. He looked me right in the eyes and there was a deep knowing of one another. I went over, picked him up, talked to him and held him. He looked at me and he was breathing but you could tell he was hurt very badly. I kept on repeating 'Timmy, the Lord is good. God loves us, Jesus is here' and God was there with us. The peace of God was there with us. If anyone doubts the reality of heaven or doubts the reality of the living God in their most difficult times, GOD IS THERE.

The accident happened near the front yard of a Christian family in Pollocksville, North Carolina. The emergency service was called right away. When the ambulance man arrived Timothy was still alive, but a few minutes later he died in my arms and went into the presence of the Lord. God is real and there's no time, no place, no situation that God is not with us. So I share just these two events.

My wife passed through a very deep period of grief. My son David also went through a long time of grief, guilt and condemnation. I was under condemnation also. I have been a pastor for more than seventeen years. I've counselled people who have lost loved ones and I've talked about grief and quoted verses and tried to comfort. I've lost my own father and relatives, but until this happened I never really understood grief.

I understand C. S. Lewis' *A Grief Observed* better now. He was a great man who wrote so many books, and comforted so many people. Then when his own wife died he went into a deep depression. It's not a question of weakness of faith or of not being right with God, but grieving can be so heavy, no matter how strong your faith is. My wife had a long battle. My struggle was not quite so long—we are all made differently—but from that first day it was just as if something had been ripped out of my heart.

No condemnation

I received a call from a close friend, a missionary in Mexico. He had heard about Timothy's death and called to comfort me. He prayed for me over the phone and a tremendous weight was lifted from my heart when he began to intercede in the Spirit for me. After his call I went to the Bible and opened it, without searching, at Job 1:8. It said, 'Hast thou considered my servant Job, a perfect man, an upright man, who feareth God and escheweth evil?' and the Lord said, 'That's how I see you: I see you as my servant. You are not guilty, not responsible for the death of your son.' I have not had one moment of guilt since reading that scripture. The devil has tried to put that on me again but I say, 'Hast thou considered my servant Job, a perfect and upright man who feareth God and escheweth evil?' So I don't receive the guilt.

I acknowledge that decisions that I made that day could have been wiser concerning the trip and the accident, but I trust that God is a sovereign God; He does all things well. Timothy's death was not good in one sense, but in another sense God permits everything according to his good and perfect will and he turns all things to good. A. S. Worley came up to me on the day of Timothy's funeral and said, 'I believe God has a word for you: "As for God, his way is perfect; the word of the Lord is tried: he is a buckler to all them that trust in him".'

Mary continues:

Prior to Timothy's death, as a mother, I could enter partially into the heartbreak of mothers who had over and over cried out to the Lord for their sons' and daughters' deliverance from drugs. We sometimes had to tell the mothers to throw them out of the house. As long as they had a bed to sleep in and food on the table, they 'had it made'. That is a hard decision for a mother to make. But I have never talked to anyone who has done it and regretted it.

But then on July 19, 1991 God allowed the greatest tragedy of our personal lives. I became a bereaved mother. Our youngest son Timothy, at nine years of age, was killed in a car accident. We were home on furlough in the States for a much needed rest. My world came crashing in on me. My life changed forever. But I want to say God *did not* let this happen so that 'Mary Tepper could relate better to the mothers in Betel'. God is not like that.

At the end of August, 1991 we were to return to Spain. Elliott and the three boys wanted to return. I knew I was not ready, but I could not bear to be separated from the family that was left to me. I told Elliott that I would go back, but only as a wife and mother. The Tepper Hotel was going to be closed down until further notice. I could not face participating in the ministry. I needed lots of room, and I took it—to save my own sanity.

The people in Betel did not know what to do with me. The mothers couldn't bear to see me, the missionary, in so much pain. But I was a very normal mother. What else could I feel?

Grace in the midst of grief

People from both conservative and charismatic backgrounds, whom I thought walked closely with the Lord, rebuked me for bitterness, anger and unforgiveness when I was only weeks into my grief. Others just ignored me. After being battered around by judgement and condemnation, I withdrew from everyone and waited on God, asking him to send those who would love me, affirm me, and accept me. He sent three people from the States during that first year—Melinda Fish being the first, then Ruth Deir, and latterly Paul Johansson.

At first Melinda was the only one who could handle the honest expression of my own feelings and struggles. She was writing a book called *Restoring the Wounded Woman* and was going to include a chapter on grief. She asked if she could write about my grief and I said 'yes'. After I received the manuscript for correction, I had the courage to talk in public for the first time since Timothy had died. I shared with the Betel church a little of what I had felt and thought during the previous eleven months.

It took me a long time to be able to trust people again and to develop a new relationship with God. I began attending an English Bible study with women I had never known before, women who did not know me as 'Mary the missionary' and had no expectations of me. They loved me as I was, and poured oil into my gaping wounds.

My first step back into Betel was to rejoin the worship group. It was definitely more by faith than by feelings. This I did during the first year of my grief. During the second year I began to take over the leadership of a Thursday morning prayer meeting with the other lady missionaries and the wives of our Spanish leaders. I also began to attend the Friday morning pastors' meeting.

Now, in my third year since Timothy died, I have had to take over the leadership of the women's Bible study again, and I have begun to travel with Elliott to some of the centres outside of Madrid so that I can spend time with the wives of our leaders. I am so glad to be a part of the Betel family.

7

EAR TO THE HEART OF GOD

Elliott continues:

Faith — hearing and doing

Faith comes by hearing and hearing by the word of God. I am not talking about the popular concept of faith—the 'name it and claim it' kind. You can't speak the word of faith until you have heard the word of faith, because God is the originator of faith. His Spirit *is* the Spirit of faith. We may in our human efforts try to imitate him, but it doesn't work unless God speaks. God will do what he wants to do when he wants to do it. The key for manifesting the spirit of faith is hearing what God is saying.

In Galatians Paul asks the question, 'He that worketh miracles among you, does he do it by works of the law or by the hearing of faith?' Much of the literature I have read tends to imply that a simple mechanical 'speaking' of faith will result in miracles, but they can only be done after the hearing of faith and then by the word of faith.

So I have simply tried to put my ear to the heart of God. The secret of Betel is walking in union with Christ, abiding in Christ, walking in divine consciousness. It's simply being part of the divine mind and then being his hands and his feet for the expansion of his will. If you can find out what God's doing and do it, it will work. If you try to do something God's not doing, he may permit you to have some success, some fruit, but it will never be quite the same.

This was confirmed for me about three years ago when I was visiting Norman Grubb. From my days as a candidate

I've always had a close relationship with him and he has always encouraged us, prayed for us, and been our champion. We love and honour him. It was his book on C. T. Studd that drew me into WEC.

One day I said to him, 'Brother Grubb, I have a very hard time in some prayer meetings because I just don't sense faith in many of the prayers. I say that humbly, not critically; we have lists and we pray over them but there is little faith in it.' He replied, 'It is so easy just to pray, pray, pray, when really all you have to do is hear the voice of God, then go and do it.' I said, 'That's what we do! We hear the voice of God and then we go and do it.' Now Mr. Grubb was not belittling intercessory prayer. He wrote *Rees Howells, Intercessor!* But like all true intercession it will lead to action; the invisible becomes the visible.

Tuning in and moving on

Before our work started to develop I was very much an intercessor; I could spend hours in prayer and hours in the word; in fact people used to think I had a problem—I tuned out too much, I was too heavenly-minded. That was one of the great criticisms of me in Bible School. I could spend the whole day with the Lord and I'd be perfectly happy. But once you are in tune, once you are in phase, once the Cross brings you to the place where your self-life is broken and God can really flow through you, it's not difficult for him to gain your attention. You don't have to spend as much time being still. You can move in the purpose of God.

In Betel, God speaks to us; we hear him and we go. We pray along the way; we breathe prayers; we live prayers, we are a prayer. And that revelation, if you call it a revelation, or that method, if you call it a method, has been imparted to the Betel leadership.

We have young Christians just two or three years old in

the Lord who have very bad backgrounds—some of them are semi-literate—and yet they can hear the voice of God and they can actually manifest the spirit of faith and bring the invisible into the visible. That is the secret of Betel.

I believe that we've been able to impart this principle because it was imparted to us. I have to acknowledge A. S. Worley as a man who imparted that spirit of faith to me. And there are others like Costa Deir, Paul Johansson, and Norman Grubb. I've sensed that same spirit of faith in the great Christian biographies that I've read, such as George Mueller, Hudson Taylor and C. T. Studd. It's in Rees Howell's life and it's in all the great missionaries and men and women of God who have done mighty things for him. They've taken hold of the spirit of faith, or rather, the Spirit of faith has taken hold of them. It's nothing new. It's just trying to return to the apostolic pattern, the apostolic spirit.

Men who helped me

I have really to thank three men in Spain who have helped me greatly. The first is Daniel Del Vecchio, he is my example; he's really the grandfather of the rehabilitation ministry in Spain. I think everyone has to acknowledge that he had the first viable Christian centres. They started in Torremolinos and Málaga about twenty years ago during the 'Jesus People' movement when international hippies were flowing through Spain down into Morocco on the drug trail. He had come from Cuba and Mexico where he had established a very successful ministry. He preached the gospel in Cholula Puebla, Mexico, the town where we started our first work, where the Amistad Christian Church is today. In fact he told me that some Mexicans had tried to burn them alive by throwing gasoline on a bus which they were using in Cholula.

Daniel's vision affected me in two ways. He had a vision

of God working in Spain among the outcasts, the drug addicts, the prostitutes and the alcoholics. He moved to fulfil that vision by trying to rescue them, providing refuges and homes, and by preaching the gospel to them when most of the church in Spain were uninterested.

Secondly he also saw God providing for that work through Christian businesses. He had a vision in which he saw seven full years and then seven lean years, and God told him to prepare for the seven lean years by making the communities self-sufficient. So he began a number of farms. He has a large herd of dairy cattle. He has a cheese factory. He grows sweetcorn and distributes it throughout the country. He also at one time had a bakery. He involved his people in practical work and began to provide for his community through their own self-help businesses. Daniel became the founder of REMAR in Spain. He has changed the name of his work to 'INDUSTRIAS REALES'.

Then Miguel Diez, one of his disciples, started REMAR of 'PAIS VASCO' (Basque country) in Vitoria. The Vitoria-based work soon grew bigger than the 'mother' organisation and has spread throughout Spain. Today they have missions in Chicago, in Latin America, Portugal and Switzerland. Miguel perfected Daniel's vision. He started the first second-hand stores in Spain.

The third influence that I have to acknowledge is Ray Pollnow. Ray is an American with the Missionary Revival Crusade. I met him in my first month or two in Mexico; he had been involved with two other missionaries in the formation of a group of about 100 churches in the Oaxaca and Guerrero states of Mexico. Ray has always been a very romantic kind of figure, an adventurer. He lived in Tlaxiaco where they had an airstrip and planes. They used to drop tracts over a large portion of southern Mexico and they would fly into small mountain airstrips and preach to the indigenous peoples. Ray was used greatly by the Lord to bring the gospel to these remote peoples.

I didn't spend a lot of time with Ray, but the few trips that I did make with him into the mountains greatly influenced me. I saw an apostolic missionary preaching the gospel just as it was preached in the book of Acts. I count Ray as a natural genius, although he was an uneducated man with a minimum of Bible training. He used to say that his greatest ambition in life was to own a junk yard and to run a service station! Actually he was a builder; he built houses commercially. He's a very handy, practical man, with a deep discernment and a tremendous gift of faith. Just to be in his presence was an inspiration.

He influenced me as a young missionary and I picked up from him probably more than anyone else the principle of individual discipleship. He discipled men 'along the way'. He didn't do it by sending them to Bible School, or by sitting them down in a church and teaching them. He took them alongside him and let them accompany him as he preached the gospel. He trained leaders this way and allowed them to function and minister as they were growing up. He didn't wait till they were 'mature'. He allowed them to do things as they grew and corrected them in the process. He also had a gift: he could testify to people, lead them to the Lord and give such a revelation of Christ that they could go on and almost immediately be church planters. Some of his early disciples in the mountains of Oaxaca and Guerrero began preaching the gospel from the day of their conversion— often with 'signs following' and a great ingathering of converts. He had many people like that. He had a way of making that kind of impact in the depths of someone's spirit. I really wanted to be like Ray. He's not a perfect fellow. He has faults and people don't understand him, but he has unique gifts.

Ray hated 'religion'. He attempted to avoid all religious forms and tried to re-define the essence of the gospel without old forms; for example, he won't let his people use the word 'brother' or 'sister', he won't let them use 'hallelujah' or 'amen', because they have become clichés without meaning. I am glad he is now working in Spain. He continues to be a help and inspiration to me.

Faith — something from nothing

Faith creates something from nothing when God reveals his will. He speaks out of eternity. He speaks the words that create the visible from the invisible. Faith comes by hearing the word of God and by listening. It also comes by seeing. God may reveal in vision, in dreams. There are many ways he gives us a revelation: through the written word, audibly or visually. What that means to me is that we have to begin to see and hear with the inner man, to see and hear with the heart, to see with the eyes of the new man and with the mind of Christ. We have to dissociate ourselves from the 'old man' and begin to discern things spiritually. Once that really happens then creativity is natural; it just flows.

8

THE KEY TO STABILITY: DISCIPLESHIP IN DEPTH

A work that is not grounded firmly in biblical truth will never survive the counter attacks of the enemy, so from the earliest days of Betel there has always been a strong thrust towards giving adequate training to those showing signs of spiritual growth and seriousness of purpose.

One of the key figures in this area has been Paul Anderson. The son of a Canadian Pentecostal Holiness pastor, he came to the Lord at the tender age of eight and at eighteen entered the Elim Bible Institute in New York State. He served the Lord first in Cuba where he was joined by Doris whom he had met while at Elim. They were married in 1958. After the Cuban revolution they moved to Colombia where they served as valued members of the WEC team, teaching at its Bible School near Bogota. In 1973 they moved back to Elim where Paul was Director of the Elim Foreign Missions Department for a number of years. In 1986 the call of God took them to Spain where they have had a close relationship with the Betel team. Paul has made an immense contribution to the work and is recognised by mission agencies throughout Spain as a biblical scholar who has a superb mastery of Spanish.

Paul takes up the story:

From the earliest days of Betel we all recognised the need to spend time teaching the young people who were saved from the drug culture, especially those who were obviously potential leaders. Elliott and I did some teaching on a rather sporadic basis, and I led a group through a New Testament survey using TEE (Theological Education by Extension) materials. But it was apparent that we needed to do something in a consistent way.

While we were back in the States in 1988, Elliott wrote to me about his desire to start a school within the framework of Betel and asked me to serve as its director; this I was happy to do, because my vision in Spain was the training of national workers.

When we arrived back, Elliott, Armando García of Mexico and I met to consider the project and make plans for the opening of a school in January, 1989. But what would we call it? Elliott suggested 'The Adullam Bible School' because the Cave of Adullam (1 Sam. 22:1-2) was the place where the outcasts of Israel identified with David and were transformed under his influence to be worthy leaders in the nation.

But how were we to construct a programme that was adequate, yet would not interfere with the ongoing practical activities of the centres? A pattern emerged: we divided the school year into five modules of eight weeks each and worked out a curriculum that covered basic subjects such as Introduction to the Old Testament, Introduction to the New Testament, Doctrine, Personal Evangelism, Cults, Hermeneutics, Ethics, Eschatology and Church History, plus special courses on key New Testament books like Romans and Acts.

We had classes four days a week to start with, but this proved impractical because it took the leaders away too much from the routine work of the centres. We changed to two days a week and with three hours of classes each day. We also moved to three modules of ten weeks each year. Latterly we have added advanced courses for those who have covered the basics.

The students are selected by the Betel leadership group. They must be converts with at least one year's Christian experience. Classes have been held in the various church locations that Betel has used in Madrid.

As I look over the list of twelve students who constituted the first group in 1989, ten of them are still actively involved in the work of Betel, and some of these are leading Betel developments overseas. Almost all of these were rescued from drugs and crime and are real trophies of the grace of God. Of subsequent groups, probably an average of 80% are still involved in the work. This is due, in part, to the fact that they have to show potential as future workers before being admitted to the course.

Of course this is not the only teaching input they receive. All must attend the two main church meetings on Friday nights and Sunday mornings when up to an hour of solid Bible teaching is given. There is a central leaders' gathering on a Monday night.

There are Wednesday evening meetings and morning devotional sessions held at all centres. Practical experience in evangelism takes place at weekends and there are open air meetings in the parks during the warmer months. All of these, plus daily contact in the community lifestyle, give the participants a well-rounded training and valuable practical experience.

As we look back over the five years of Adullam's existence, the results are thrilling. All who have invested time and effort in its operation feel well rewarded as we see Spanish nationals becoming 'able ministers of the New Covenant'.

Since Betel's goal is the raising up of strong national churches, attention is given to teaching at all levels. Betel's first women's group was started in Madrid in August of

1985 by Mary Tepper and Laura Silva, a short-term Mexican missionary from Elim Bible Institute. Subsequently Myk Hall, Mary, and Doris Anderson have taken the leadership at different times over the years.

Doris describes a typical gathering:

The meetings consist of worship in song followed by a Bible lesson. Then at the end there is a time of prayer in which requests from the women are taken up. It is not uncommon for tears to be shed as they intercede for one another and especially for a son or daughter going through the Betel programme. Sometimes it is this kind of praying that touches the hearts of unsaved visitors.

Because most participants in the Betel programmes are usually single and in their twenties, and because their parents are in their forties and fifties, there are not many children in the churches compared to the total number attending. However there is a real sensitivity to the needs of the little ones in the fellowship. At the start Mary Tepper took care of them on her own but later other mothers joined her, and eventually Doris Anderson and her sixteen-year-old daughter, Gloria, had a vital contribution. Doris also took on the task of training potential Sunday School teachers from among recent converts and almost all of these are now active in the Lord's work. For Juan Carrasco, leader in Barcelona, and Tito, leader in New York, their first venture in Christian communication was teaching Sunday School in the Betel church. More recently the children's ministry has blossomed under the capable leadership of Lola Pino, with valuable assistance from Raúl Reyes and Sara Flores, single workers from Mexico, as well as national helpers.

THE RESCUE PROCESS

1

FROM CHAOS TO CONTENTMENT
The story of Luis and Lola Pino

'Where's the gold?' he bellowed, thrusting me hard against the police car. Pistol in hand, the undercover narcotics agent kept insisting, 'Where is it? Where is it?' At that moment my partner, already handcuffed, screamed out, 'Luis, give it to them! They know everything!'

I was cornered, so I reluctantly climbed the stairs to my apartment and brought out the stolen jewels, handing them over to the two policemen. Immediately they arrested me and escorted me to the local police station where I was roughly pushed into a dark cell. This was my reward for accepting stolen goods as payment for drugs!

Luis Pino left school at thirteen and later began work as an apprentice fitter and locksmith. Lacking paternal discipline because his father had died when he was only three, he was easily led by his teenage peers into smoking tobacco and then 'pot'. The next step was selling it and reaping a handsome profit. He describes the sequence of events after that.

My life began to gather momentum at a frightening rate as I moved from hashish to freaking out on acid trips, later sniffing cocaine and morphine.

At the age of eighteen I tried 'mainlining' with heroin and was immediately convinced that finally I had found the answer to my long search for happiness—it made me feel so relaxed, and reduced all my problems to insignificance. However, I soon discovered that the more heroin I consumed the more I needed. Financially it was ruining me, so I accepted an offer from a 'pusher' to sell it for him on the streets. In no time I was making huge profits, which in turn was spent on my own habit—each 'fix' sending all my problems away ... or so it seemed.

So here I was, at 19, in this cold dark cell. For the first time in my life I began to go through the agonies of withdrawal. At first I didn't know what they were, because I'd always had an abundant supply of the 'white powder'. When the pains got more than I could bear I desperately scraped some white plaster from the wall in an attempt to convince myself that it was the thing that my mind and body longed for, but in the end I tipped it out on the floor in disgust.

Three days later, after having faced a preliminary trial, I was transferred to the main Madrid prison which houses 2,600 male prisoners—twice the number for which it was originally constructed. By the time I was shown to my cell, the withdrawal pains had reached their peak. I was feeling bad—really bad—but beyond the physical anguish was a deep sense of being punished, knowing that I deserved it all.

Even though I gradually grew accustomed to prison life, it didn't cease to be a dangerous place. I had to be continually on the lookout for those who would sexually abuse me or steal whatever I had. At times I had to fight for my life in order to maintain a place in the established 'pecking order', but then violence is a way of life when you're 'inside'. Each day that dawned I woke longing to be set free from those walls and to try my luck on the streets again. This time I was sure I would do it 'right' and not be caught.

After two months I was released on bail. My girlfriend, Lola, and another dealer had been set free just a week previously so they, with two other friends, came to pick me up. As I walked through the prison gates there was just one thing on my mind—a 'fix'. Even though, having been through withdrawal, I was not physically dependent on heroin, my head kept telling me that that was what I needed.

We walked across the street and entered a bar. In the restroom I shot up with the drugs my friends had brought. Only minutes after obtaining my freedom I was celebrating with a needle in my vein.

Luis returned to his old job as a fitter, but it was not long till he was dismissed for stealing. Other jobs came up, but all ended the same way. He returned to trafficking but his own demands outstripped his profits. It was like being on a train that kept going faster and faster. His only recourse was robbery. He describes what happened after he married Lola.

After our marriage we had a little son, Luisete, but due to my addiction to heroin I behaved as though my family did not exist. I would often stay away all night. They never knew when I would turn up. Furthermore I was becoming weaker and weaker. I tried to grab a handbag from a lady in the street, but she turned out to be stronger than I and put up such a fight that I had to run off without it. That was when I decided to sell packets of tissues to passing motorists at intersections.

One day at the stoplights it was raining heavily and I was saturated. Not surprisingly, I had not sold anything. Feeling depressed and absolutely destitute I stood there numbed, staring blankly at the road. My eyes lighted on a soggy leaflet covered in mud lying in the gutter. I reached down and picked it up; it was advertising a Christian drug rehabilitation centre called Centro Betel.

What drew my attention was the fact that admission was free. By this time I was so wet through that I decided to leave selling and head home. When I arrived I showed the leaflet to Lola who, being even more desperate than I, immediately rang the number and made an appointment for me.

100

After being admitted, I was surprised to find other fellows like myself, some of whom I had known from my drug trafficking days. They had swapped the needle for the Bible and were sharing with me how Jesus had transformed their lives. Having known what they were like before, I was astounded at the incredible change in them. It affected everything they said and did. I longed for what they had.

This time the withdrawal symptoms were not too severe but they were lengthy. (I had used the money from the sale of tissues to buy fixes rather than food.) I did not sleep for fifteen nights. The other men prayed for me and told me: 'You need to cry to God until you do it from your heart.' So that's what I did night after night, really without conviction that anything would happen.

One day I was lying in bed suffering from cramps and crying to God. Suddenly I felt heat, as if a fire had started to burn through my body. I wondered what was happening but soon fell asleep. When I wakened it was as if the Lord was confirming that he was doing a powerful work in me, but I really did not fully understand. I continued like this for about three months. Lola was at home with my son and I continued in the centre.

One day Elliott took me to a meeting at a seminary and said, 'I want you to get up and give your testimony.' I responded, 'Elliott, I can't get up and give a testimony, I haven't decided to follow Christ.' He said, 'Well, just say what's been happening to you since you came.'

I got up, thinking about Lola because we needed 5,000 pesetas to pay the rent on our little house. She was there at home, thinking about entering the centre and leaving her job, and she didn't have the money for this payment. So I stood up and said, 'Well, I've been off drugs now for more than two months and I feel much better physically. I'm in a Christian centre and they're treating me well.' Spiritually I really didn't know what to say because there was still this veil in front of me. I did explain to them that I was still seeking Christ and if anyone wanted to pray for me they were welcome, so a group of students and older folks came around and did so. I sat down and Elliott began to preach.

An old woman, whom I'd never seen before, came and sat next to me. She discreetly put some paper into my hand, closed it, and said, 'Here's something that God has told me to give you.' She got up and walked away and I opened my hand. She had given me a gift of money and it wasn't 3,000 pesetas, or 6,000 pesetas: it was exactly 5,000 pesetas! Through that incident God again showed me his power.

It wasn't long before I cried out to Jesus to forgive me for all the wrong I had done and begged him to deliver me from the many chains in my life. He did! After three months I was baptised.

Being something of an introvert, Luis went on rather quietly with the Lord, and was not given much responsibility. He noted how others who were more outgoing seemed to be given more authority, but that had its dangers and he saw several fall. He was content to grow steadily and, little by little, his personality started to change. He became more purposeful, more direct, and more goal-orientated. He says about himself:

As I grew steadily I was entrusted with money. This made me nervous. Previously when I saw money I would grab it and run, but gradually a sense of responsibility and authority started to develop. Before, I did not have enough grip to run my own family life; nowadays I have to organise and exert authority over hundreds in the centres. Before, I did not have the memory to take care of my own situations, now I have to control a number of departments.

102

Before, money was a number one problem; today millions of pesetas pass through my hands. It is all by God's grace and goodness.

Now we need to hear Lola's side of the story.

'Pack your things and clear out of this house! People would hardly believe you had a son! All you ever think about is the next fix! Well, I'm fed up with you! Get out of here and leave us in peace!' I pointed to the door. Luis snatched his jacket from the coat rack and left. As the door clicked shut I slumped into the nearest armchair numbed by my own words. The same old questions flooded my mind. What a nightmare of a marriage! Where had the romance and the happiness gone?

From the age of twelve all that mattered to me was having a good time. My life consisted of going from one party to the next, accompanied by the many friends I had gathered around me. Together we smoked and drank the hours away.

Just the same, I just couldn't shake off an inner yearning to find peace and freedom. That desire led to a developing relationship with some hippie friends. They seemed to be just what I'd been searching for. So, I began to dress as they did, accompanying them to their rock festivals and taking their drugs, believing that my heart cries would soon be satisfied.

One day I met a fellow named Luis. We became close and together enjoyed sniffing, and later mainlining, cocaine or heroin at weekends. We were very much in love, and life had never been so fantastic. We didn't need much 'powder' at first, so we could afford the weekly luxury. However, as our requirements increased to daily doses, we decided we'd have to take up selling the stuff to pay for our fixes. What a deadly trap! Before we knew it we were shooting up every bit of powder we had, leaving none to sell. We now mainlined, not to be 'high', but just to feel 'normal.'

Luis and I were married in 1984 and then had a son. Yes! Under those conditions! Understandably, fights and screaming matches characterised our union. Although we shared the same bed, we found ourselves in two completely different worlds: his, one of crime and delinquency, and mine, one of fear and frustration. I struggled constantly with feelings of hatred towards my husband, yet, at the same time I worried myself sick about him. I don't know how many times we reached the point of going our separate ways, tired of the hell in which we were trapped. But to whom could I go with a baby son? Besides, Luis couldn't bring himself to abandon us. So our nightmare of a marriage continued for several long, anguish-filled years.

Lola was relieved when Luis decided to go to Betel, but she felt no need to follow. With a struggle she managed to wean herself off heavy drugs. She would often stay up half the night going through withdrawal and frequently took tranquillisers to help her—all this on top of working a normal day and caring for the boy. But loneliness took its toll. She describes how she coped:

I often left my son with my parents and spent late evenings with friends, smoking 'joints' and having an occasional drink, but despite having friends and seeing some light at the end of the tunnel, I was still frustrated and unfulfilled.

I used to attend the meetings at Betel church because Luis would be there. But I was bored and kept looking at my watch. Every time I looked at Luis he would have his head bent forward and his eyes closed. I would bend down, look into his face, and think, 'This fellow is crazy.'

After he had been there a while I became really exasperated. I thought to myself, 'Here I am surrounded by friends and a caring family, living at home with my son, and making enough money, yet I am so depressed and miserable. Meanwhile, he's got nothing, and yet I've never seen him so happy. "God! If what Luis has been trying to explain to me is really true, prove it to me by getting me out of this mess!"'

An argument with my parents brought things to a head. I was always leaving little Luis with them, and they started to resent it. We had a big fight one night and when I came home I lay on the bed and said, 'If this stuff Luis is telling me about Jesus is really true, I'm going to go to Betel and see if it will work for me.'

It took me about a week to settle all my finances, pay off the rent, get rid of the dog, and resign from my job. After checking that I could take little Luis with me I went over to Betel and they placed us in the first girls' house in Vicálvaro.

Things went surprisingly smoothly for me. I entered into the Betel lifestyle and gradually I became aware of the decision I had to make about accepting Christ as Lord. After seeing Luis baptised I came to a crisis point. I had to decide whether to stay or go. And I knew that to stay meant accepting Christ. The centre and God were the same to me.

I can't remember a specific day or a specific event that could be described as my conversion. I had asked the Lord several times for forgiveness, but I remember that my decision to stay was in effect my decision for Christ. Myk Hall and another girl, Estrella, just kept feeding me with the word of God, and gradually I came to a place of assurance.

Luis and Lola have moved on steadily to maturity and to responsibility. In fact, Luis today is carrying the major load in the running of Betel Madrid, both in terms of organisation and of financial management. He gives a further testimony regarding the Lord's provision for him and Lola:

After I had been at Betel a year and a half, and Lola a year, we felt it would be good to move back to our little house. Actually we had found paying the rent quite a financial hurdle, so when a good job in my trade became available, everything seemed just right. But I asked Raúl and Elliott for their opinion. I was surprised when they both said we should not leave under pressure—the pressure to find rent money and the pressure to be on our own as a family again.

We decided to stay and trust God about the house. It was beautiful to see how he provided for us. My mother, when she visited us, would always give me 200 pesetas 'for drinks' but I put that aside for the rent. God met the need somehow, every time.

Once, my grandmother, who had never written to me in nine years, sent 2,000 pesetas and that was exactly what we needed to complete the rent money.

As far as responsibility is concerned, this has come to me bit by bit as other senior workers have left to take up other duties. I have never really wanted it but it has just kept coming. It is all simply a matter of the Lord's grace.

Lola concludes:

Six years of costly refining have gone by since then. Everything is entirely different! The Lord has moulded my husband into a wonderful man, whom I now love and respect. He has turned our marriage into the closest relationship possible. The Lord has given us a little daughter and a special love for both of our children. Above all, he has dealt with my dominating personality and the mountain of emotional hurts I once had.

Our home is transformed, because in Jesus Christ I have at last discovered the peace and freedom for which I had searched for so long.

2

HEROIN'S SLAVES SET FREE
The story of Juan Carlos and Mariluz

That winter's night in 1986, two of us climbed a store roof and pried open the skylight. We were desperate. I lowered my legs through the opening into the darkness and groped for something solid to stand on. In a flash, I was in the air and on the ground—a distance of some ten metres. Pain shot up my legs as the store alarm howled. In panic, I grabbed several hams from a shelf, scrambled up a tower of wooden pallets, out through a hole in the roof, and down to the ground. The pain was unbearable. I knew my feet were broken, but there was no time to worry about that now. The police were approaching. My friend slung me over his shoulder, hid me in a nearby ditch, and dashed off to exchange the stolen goods for heroin. At last we had our next fix.

For the next two months I had to stay at home. Unable to walk, with my feet in plaster casts, I forced my mother to coax morphine prescriptions from a local doctor.

I spent nearly ten years in Madrid living through episodes like that. Heroin was my god. My habits, my work, in fact my whole life revolved around this powder and the needle.

From a young age Juan Carlos could recall being more rebellious than normal, as though a driving force was continually urging him to do evil—anything that was prohibited.

At fourteen he began to mix with the different gangs in

the East Madrid neighbourhood and was soon smoking hashish. Shortly after, he was dealing in it, along with amphetamines, acid and eventually all types of drugs. With each drug his will-power gradually weakened. Unable to cope with the demands of a regular job, he would just give up or be fired.

By age nineteen he was snorting heroin. Then at age twenty-one he gave himself to it body and soul, knowing that each time he shot up it was draining his life little by little. The means of obtaining it no longer mattered. He was into armed robbery, hold-ups, even stealing from his own family and neighbours. His obsession completely negated the few scruples he had.

Over the years, he tried to break the habit several times with the help of his family, using sleeping pills. He even left Madrid looking for 'escape routes', seeking jobs on ships that would carry him overseas, or working up in the northern mountains as a lumberjack, but to no avail.

Finally, at twenty-nine, ill and living on the street like a beggar, he was given the address of Betel in Madrid by some friends.

Juan Carlos describes the early days at the centre:

I had one vivid impression after being admitted in November, 1986—LOVE. Instead of finding a prison-like atmosphere, I met people who were genuinely interested in me and wanted to care for me.

The withdrawal period was painful. I did not sleep for fifteen nights; my bones hurt; my mouth and nose were running constantly, but the staff gave me light work to occupy my mind. After ten days my 'shadow' (a personal monitor assigned to accompany recovering addicts during their first months of rehabilitation) went to make a phone call. I found myself alone so I took his clothes and ran out to the street. I went back to my old haunts but I felt a terrible anxiety and emptiness. I began to smoke and drink, telling myself I would not take drugs again, but the feelings intensified so I found two pushers and shot up twice.

But amazingly, these fixes did nothing for me—I didn't feel a thing. I was so frustrated I went straight back to Betel. It was as though a veil had been pulled away from my eyes. I saw clearly what drug addiction was; I cut my ties with the past and with street life—that was the end of it.

My conversion came through a series of steps. First I started to feel bad when I lied or talked about sex, or swore. Then I kept asking God to do something powerful in my life—to change me. The next step was when I read a book about a revival in Canada. It talked about loving your neighbour, repentance and forgiveness. Something happened inside me; it was like an explosion in my heart. I felt completely full of the love of God, and joy. I could feel in the depths of my being what the Bible calls 'rivers of living water'. I could feel Jesus; his Spirit was inside me, in my heart. The days went by and I began to feel new sensations. Love flowed out from me to others. I couldn't lie any more. There was no more hate or bitterness. I had communion with God, the Creator of this world. It was fantastic.

Mariluz was typical of the rebelliousness that engulfed Spanish youth in the eighties. Here is her story:

My father was an engineer in telecommunications so we were comfortably well off. But at sixteen I started taking amphetamines and by seventeen I had a boyfriend and became pregnant. I left home soon after and was married. My husband was a member of a gang and was totally undisciplined. He drank a lot and spent all our money—I didn't even have enough to feed the baby—so I left him and

109

went home. After three years I heard he had changed so I went back to him, but he was as bad as ever, drinking, using drugs and going with other women, and in less than a year I left him again, taking our daughter with me. I went to live with my sister.

It was during this time that I managed to get a job as a waitress. I met up with a fellow called Jesús who was hooked on heroin. He persuaded me to take it and we started to live together in a flat. I came down with a bad case of hepatitis, then he became sick, so we both lost our jobs.

We took to dealing in drugs and were receiving unemployment benefits, but even with all that money we didn't have enough to satisfy our craving for heroin. Eventually we had to sell our furniture.

Things became so bad that we felt our only hope of breaking free was to separate. My sister knew of someone who was planning to go to Betel, so she called and asked if I could be admitted and they agreed.

When I entered I had no idea what a Christian was. But it didn't matter. All I wanted to do was break free of drugs. At first everything sounded strange and my first reaction was to cry and cry, out of self pity, telling myself, 'Look where you've ended up now.' It was all so strange to me. I felt that I was in the hands of some crank religious 'sect'. I had no knowledge that Christian drug rehabilitation centres even existed.

I passed through withdrawal and, little by little, began to become interested in the things that they spoke about, such as love, mercy, peace, joy, and the patience of God.

My companions were girls who had gone through the same experiences I had, but were now different. At first I couldn't believe that they had been drug addicts. I thought they were just faking. I saw they were healthy, happy, and helping one another. For me these things had ceased to exist.

110

I no longer knew what it was to be happy.

As time passed, I became well physically. I had been there four months, when one day during a meeting, the person who was speaking said that if any wanted to change their lives and give themselves to the Lord Jesus, he could exchange the old for the new: happiness in place of bitterness, love in place of hate, joy in place of sadness. I felt an inward impulse and went forward. From that day my life changed. Jesus began to live inside me.

The new life in Christ is wonderful, but growth has to take place and one of the areas in which Mariluz had trouble was relationships. She describes how the Lord brought her through to victory:

I didn't get along well with a certain girl in the centre and when, one day, someone had to accompany me to the hospital (I had a skin ailment), the leader of the residence purposely sent this person with me. I was so angry I felt like leaving, but while I was waiting for her one of our men handed me a New Testament. I opened it and began to read these words: 'Anyone who does not love his brother whom he has seen cannot love God whom he has not seen' (1 John 4:20).

Then we had to leave. All the way to hospital, all the time there and all the way home I didn't say a word to her. But the question flooding my mind was, 'How can I put this situation right? How can I ask her to forgive me?' Finally I said, 'Stop,' and there and then asked her forgiveness. We talked and hugged each other. That incident broke something in me and since then I've never felt hate towards anyone.

Juan Carlos made great strides at Betel and his consistent testimony gave the staff grounds for increasing his responsibility. Mariluz describes the start of their relationship:

Juan Carlos and I started to feel drawn towards each other, but there were problems. I had not yet legally terminated my marriage to my previous husband, so we discontinued our friendship since, in Betel, married individuals are not permitted to pursue other relationships. In the meantime I was asked to serve at our Cuenca centre.

My husband did not want God or reconciliation and his immorality gave me grounds for a biblical divorce—but that took a long time. That whole experience of waiting was a time of struggle for Juan Carlos and me, but it led to spiritual depth and growth. At times we thought of giving up and just taking off together; but we knew that God wanted us to serve him, so we waited and did not take any short cuts. It took a year for everything to fall into place.

Juan Carlos and Mariluz are now married and living in Alcalá de Henares where they are in charge of a big centre with a hundred men. Juan Carlos is a man of ability and vision and has taken over several rundown properties, renovating them, thus providing residences and workshops.

Mariluz still has Sandra with her; she is now aged ten. She and Juan Carlos now have Lydia, who is one year old. They have a long term goal of missionary service.

THE MIRACLE OF THREE CHANGED LIVES
The story of Carlos, Marimar and Rocío

The world of Carlos crashed down around him when he was sixteen. His mother died and his father departed to live with another woman. Eight children were left at home to fend for themselves, ranging in age from twenty down to seven. It was no wonder that earlier experiences with soft drugs soon developed into deeper involvement with heroin, and by eighteen he was hooked. A drug-trafficking family business mushroomed. One brother would bring cheap hashish from Morocco, and Carlos would travel to Amsterdam to pick up heroin.

It was during these years that he met Marimar. She was the sister of a man who bought drugs from Carlos. They were married when he was twenty-three, and three years later little Clara was born. At first the marriage was stable but with both of them on heroin, things started to go wrong. Marimar took Clara and went to live with her parents; Carlos lived on the streets.

Carlos tells his own story:

I did not seek help for my addiction for many years because I always had money and did not need anything. It was only in the final two years that I became desperate, when my consumption of heroin outstripped my capacity to pay for it. Someone gave me a card about Betel but I simply put it in my pocket and forgot about it.

Just in case we were ever caught, we protected ourselves from extended jail sentences by paying off local judges. A few other pushers plus my brothers and I paid them $1000 every week. We also arranged for prostitutes to be available, and sent hams and cases of whisky.

I was caught robbing a shop using a fake pistol and was sent to jail for armed robbery. I could have spent years there but the paper work was conveniently 'lost' and I was out in two months.

After serving this sentence I went one evening with a friend to look for drugs. We met another man who said, 'I know a pusher; let's go and steal from him.' I did not realise what I was letting myself in for when I went along. We arrived at a certain spot in San Blas and my companions just grabbed the heroin and ran. I was stunned at first then I ran off too, but I fell down a set of steps.

Three pushers—two men and a girl—caught up with me and stabbed me four times as I lay at the foot of the stairs. I sat up bleeding all over and found my wrist was broken. I crawled on to the street and stopped a taxi that took me to a local clinic. From there I was taken in an ambulance to the hospital.

The staff advised Marimar of my condition because they did not expect me to survive. They decided to operate and I spent six hours in theatre. That saved my life. I had to stay for forty-five days.

By the time I was discharged my stab wounds were healing, but I still had my wrist in a plaster cast. My one thought was revenge, both against my assailants and those who had deserted me. Later, I found one of the latter but he had become blind through a drug-related disease, so I did nothing to him. I discovered that the pushers were from Valencia and had just come to Madrid for supplies, so I did not pursue them.

I continued to need so much heroin for myself that my brother broke his partnership with me. I was taking about

114

four or fives grams a day, and for the last year I was simply living on the streets, sleeping in doorways or abandoned cars or in unfinished government flats.

A drugged response

One day I remembered the Betel card, and decided to go and find out what it was like. I arrived at the shop-front office and met Raúl and Tito. I used to sell drugs to Tito, so I spoke mostly with him. They did not have space for me at the men's accommodation out at Barajas, but I started to attend the meetings at the church. Everything was strange; nothing made sense at first. In one meeting I put my hand up to receive Christ but I was so drugged I fell over the chairs. It really did not mean anything.

Finally I was admitted. I arrived dirty, with only a pair of pants and a T-shirt. They took me in, washed me and cared for me; I was so impressed. Withdrawal began and I went through the first month without sleeping. My weight then was half what it is now, but after the first fifteen days I was able to walk. Of course my sole desire was to become well and then just leave. In the early days I sneaked out to have a smoke, but on the eighteenth day I threw my tobacco away and decided to remain.

Although I do not place a lot of value on that experience in the church, after the eighteenth day I began to surprise myself. I would waken in the morning with a desire to care for others. A love for others was starting to grow in me. God was at work and I asked him for his forgiveness.

As the months went by, Carlos started to have a concern for Marimar. He visited her and told her his life was changing, but she continued to take drugs. But after much persistence he succeeded in persuading her to join Betel, and to bring Clara with her. They both lived in the women's accommo-

115

dation and he with the men. They started to feel that they were once again a family unit even though they were not actually living together. At one point she went off, but Carlos searched for her and brought her back. From then on the relationship was strong. Carlos continues:

After nearly a year we were asked to help with the start of a rehabilitation centre in another district of Madrid. We were there almost a year and this gave us the opportunity of living together as a family. It was while we were there that our second child, María, was born. We returned to Betel for three more months and then moved out into normal living. I worked for a cleaning company for six months and then became manager of another firm doing the same kind of work. I can see the Lord's hand in this because this experience gave me a vision for running a company that could give employment to ex-addicts—a kind of 'half-way house'.

But after the birth of María, Marimar's health started to decline. She knew she had the AIDS virus, but now its effects were becoming apparent. It was when we were out living on our own that the doctors told us she had three years to live. From then on life was a downward spiral for her. She had several bouts of pneumonia and was always at home with fever. It was difficult to watch her physical suffering. I knew God could raise her up but it was not his will. She passed away in February, 1992.

We switch now to pick up the story of Rocío who became the second wife of Carlos. She had a grim warning about the dangers of drug-taking. When she was fifteen, her brother, eight years older, died from an overdose of heroin. Even that event, however, did not keep her from experimenting with hashish and LSD, along with her peers. When she was eighteen she left home and, soon after, moved south to the

116

province of Andalucía where she found work among the strawberry pickers. Her new companions persuaded her to smoke heroin and it was not long before she was hooked. She continues the story from there:

I started to have a relationship with a fellow who was injecting heroin, but as the memory of my brother's death gave horror of mainlining, he agreed that we should just smoke it. We went to live with his parents, but we began to have problems because he was so aggressive. I became pregnant, and when work ran out, rather than take advantage of the generosity of his parents, I decided to return to Madrid and live with my mother till the baby arrived.

After three months I returned to my friend whose name, also, was Carlos. With our little daughter Sandra we travelled from place to place, and eventually ended up staying with my sister in Torremolinos, near Málaga. However, after a time she threw us out because she was resentful at having to maintain us while we spent whatever we earned on heroin. Carlos found work in a public relations firm, but his wages were not enough to satisfy our cravings and soon we began to rob for more money.

A cure becomes imperative
I started to pressure Carlos about the need for finding a cure. There was no future to this way of life and we had the child to consider, but he reacted badly, abusing me and hitting me. He threatened to leave me and take the child with him, absolutely refusing to give up heroin. I felt really trapped. The last straw was when we were thrown out of our apartment for failing to pay the rent.

We approached the REMAR people in Torremolinos but they were not accepting any new people. They advised us to go to Betel in Madrid. We left Sandra with my sister

117

and went north. I was accepted at Betel's women's centre in Madrid, but as we were not legally married Carlos was sent to Cuenca. He could not accept the discipline and left after four days.

I decided to stay, partly because of my desire to be cured, and partly because I wanted to escape from Carlos. I thought that perhaps after a couple of months I could pick up Sandra and then stay with my mother.

Everything was very strange at first. I hadn't a clue as to what being a Christian meant, but there was a happiness about my companions. As for me, I had even lost my desire to live. They told me that Jesus would forgive me and that's really what I needed.

After three weeks Betty, one of the workers from Mexico, asked me if I was ready to give my life to Christ. I said I believed in God but not in the personal way she was talking about. She asked, 'Do you see a difference in the girls around you?' And I said, 'Yes.' We prayed together and the truth of God's love just broke me. I began to cry and when it was all over I knew I had the peace of God in my heart.

After a while I was able to arrange for Sandra to come and live at Betel.

Marimar's death

I met Marimar at church and we became close friends. In the last few months of her life she was in hospital and different ones would visit her, even staying overnight for company. I did that on one occasion. At the time of her death I did not know her husband Carlos very well, but I felt a real compassion for the family, as anyone would in a situation like that. I had no special feelings towards Carlos, but as time went on and I saw him with the girls, I realised that something was happening between us. We would greet each other and talk, and that's how it began. After being in the centre for eighteen months we were married.

Carlos and Rocío, with the three children, continued to live outside the fellowship for some time, but were recently invited to return to Betel as staff workers. They have joined the team in Valencia and are thrilled with this development.

4

THE WAY OF TRANSGRESSORS IS HARD
The story of Loli and Miguel

This story gives an insight into the rough treatment that dealers are prepared to give those who fail to pay for their supplies. By the time they had beaten up Miguel, made a huge wound in his head, and run over him with their car, he was more than ready for hospital. But we start with his partner, Loli, whose father was a drug dealer. At fourteen she was smoking marijuana and had access to drugs because she knew where her father hid his supplies in the home. She would take small portions from time to time, but never enough to arouse his suspicion. At seventeen she left home, and with like-minded companions was soon into mainlining. After a few years of this she was absolutely desperate and decided to return home, hoping to find help.

Here is her story:

Father said to me, 'OK, I am going to help you.' His plan was to give me drugs in decreasing doses, but this did nothing for me, and ultimately we shot up together. I started to work for him. This went on for several more years.

Miguel and I first met when I was fourteen. Our families were vacationing in a camping area where there was a lake. When we came home we began going out together, but often we would quarrel and then break up for a while.

It was Miguel who first told me about Betel. He went in and stayed for three months. I would visit him, but I was still hooked and did not understand what the centre was trying to achieve. He decided to leave, and went back on to the streets. Our friendship continued, but six months later we were totally desperate, and decided that we would both go, separately, to Betel.

They were crazy — but loving

For the first sixteen days I went through withdrawal. I did not sleep for one night. The thing that kept me was the love that was shown to me, and also the fact that others were going through the same experience. Although I felt the staff people were crazy, there was something about them that attracted me. When they got up in the morning there was a smile on their faces and a joy in their hearts.

On Tuesday afternoons Myk would take us for Bible studies. I remember one time when I felt particularly good, physically—I was out of withdrawal. Suddenly I felt as if a fire was going through me. I was sweating profusely. I remember I had a smile from ear to ear that would not leave me, and from the very next morning when I woke up I had a new desire to seek God. After a few months I became a 'shadow' for other girls.

Meanwhile Miguel was sent to Cuenca. We did not write to each other, and after about a month he was brought back because his mechanical skills were needed to keep the vehicles on the road. It was about another month after that when I woke up one morning feeling, 'This relationship isn't going to work any more.' So we dropped it and went our separate ways for about two years. Looking back on it now, we think God was keeping his hand on us so that we could both grow spiritually on our own.

Things were not always rosy during that period. I had a number of crises. Once I left with Miguel, but we both came back after Miguel was almost killed by some pushers. Another time, after seven months, I decided I wanted to leave. Tito, one of the leaders said, 'No, don't go, Loli, you must stay. What the world is offering you and what God is offering you are vastly different.' I said, 'No, I've decided to go.' So I walked out the front door and suddenly I felt so small and unprotected. I started to head for the bus that would take me to the Betel girls' residence where I could pick up my things, but a verse of scripture kept coming to mind; God was saying, 'Loli, look at this world around you. All of it is going to pass away. It's all vanity.' I reached the flat and a girl was there for whom I had been responsible. I told her I was going to leave and she began to cry. I told her I didn't really want to leave but that there was a struggle going on inside me. She said, 'Please stay!' I got down on my knees before the Lord and gave myself back to Christ.

After a year in the fellowship I was made a leader in the girls' residence.

We pick up Miguel's story when, at the age of eighteen, he was working for his uncle in Madrid, putting windows into cars. By this time he was already hooked on heroin spending up to $300 a day for the three fixes that he could not do without. He describes the little 'racket' he was into:

My salary was $1,000 a month, but I increased it by stealing windows from other cars, installing them and charging the customers the price of new ones. I could have worked at this for a long time because my uncle was ignorant of what I was doing, but eventually he found out and paid me off. He gave me $6,000 in severance pay and I spent it in about three weeks.

I became involved with a gang in my neighbourhood. I never actually took part in their robberies—I was a kind of back-up man looking after their equipment. I was detained by the police several times, and once they kept me for four or five days trying to persuade me to testify against the others, but I refused. After that I started to participate in the actual robberies.

I tried to move back into normal work again, putting windows into cars, but I did not have the stamina for it and gave up after a while. I started dealing in hashish and then progressed to heroin. I would take supplies from traffickers on credit but I kept failing to pay them back. Instead I used the stuff myself.

It was while I was in this jam that I decided to try Betel—not because I wanted a cure; my real reason was that I needed to escape from these dealers who were now after my blood. After living there for three months I had a dream. I saw Loli on the street and when I tried to put my arm around her in an attempt to bring her with me to Betel, she turned into a snake.

The assault

I went off to try to find her, but instead of bringing her back I stayed away and went back to drugs again. It was during that time that I met up with the dealers to whom I owed money. It happened on a road which linked two gypsy camps where they sold drugs. They beat me up, breaking my head open with a baseball bat. (I needed fourteen stitches to repair their handiwork.) I staggered along the highway looking for help but they decided to run me over with their car. They left me lying in the middle of that busy highway, unconscious. I see the hand of God in that situation, because I could easily have been run down by trucks (it was dark), but fortunately a police car came by and they took me to a clinic. It was amazing that the police stopped because this territory near the gypsy camps is very dangerous. I came out of the clinic with a bandage round my head, still feeling the effects of the drugs as well as the beating.

The word 'Betel' kept coming to my mind and I knew

that I had to return. I started looking for Loli and when I found her I said, 'We had better go back to the centre.' Within three days we were re-admitted. I remember going in on a Tuesday and being taken to Cuenca. I woke up next morning to hear everyone singing. I thought, 'I will wait just long enough to be cured and then leave.' For the first twenty-eight days I went through withdrawal and did not sleep at all. I had bouts of feeling cold, then I had hot sweats, and hallucinations. I saw dragon-like monsters, and huge terrifying insects. I had been on drugs for nearly ten years.

During this time I felt as though I was in a terrible darkness from which I was desperate to escape, but some-one kept grabbing me, pulling me back, and saying to me, 'Get out of here, get out of here: they're going to deceive you. These people are crazy. Don't stay here.'

On the other hand the converts kept saying, 'Take a leap, take a leap of faith as though you're jumping out off a wall and someone's below to catch you.' I didn't understand this at all. I didn't know what they meant and I used to go out by the bridge in Mejorada and sit there crying out to God saying, 'God, if you're really there I want to know. If you're real come to me.'

'It's not my foot, it's my heart!'

I had a problem. I couldn't forgive my father because I had always hated him. He was always drunk and was constantly hitting me and saying, 'Get out of here.' He died when I was four months in the centre and I was happy at that because I hated him so much. Then in camp at Peña de Horeb, Jack Knowles, a visiting pastor, spoke about forgiveness. He said, 'If there's somebody here that needs to forgive their father, even though he's dead, I want to pray for you.' I had a struggle, but I stood up and went forward. He prayed for me and I still didn't feel anything. I went outside after the

124

meeting and said, 'God, if you're really there, I want to know. I want something tangible.' The next day I cut my foot very badly in the river and that was what kept me at the camp, because I was going to leave.

Two days later, on the Sunday, the speaker gave an invitation. He asked anyone who wanted to receive Christ to come forward, but every time I moved my leg, my foot started to bleed. Raúl Casto and two others saw this and said, 'Don't worry about it, we'll carry you.' They picked me up, put me on a table and moved me to the front. Paul Anderson, Raúl and Juan, from Barcelona, came over and began to pray for me. Paul thought I wanted prayer for my foot, so he prayed, 'Lord, heal his foot.' I said, 'No, it's not my foot, it's my heart. I need what everybody is talking about.' It was when they started praying for me to receive Christ that my heart broke. I felt like Jacob who had to have his hip dislocated to remove his pride so that he could find God.

After being in the centre for about four months, Miguel's progress was such that the leaders felt he should be given some responsibility. One day he had a free day to leave the centre.

With one of the other men, and away from the Christian atmosphere, he succumbed to temptation, obtained drugs, and shot up. Expecting to become really high, the very opposite happened. He had a tremendous revulsion at what had happened and felt so horrible that he began to cry. He believes God allowed this so that he could experience a total hatred of addiction. After that incident another four or five months passed before the team felt he could have responsibility again. It came when Luis Pino gave him some money —about $50—to go out on a motor cycle and buy car parts. He came back with a receipt and change, and felt really good about it. He says:

Now I carry between $200-$300 every day, and at one point I was given $5,000 to go and buy a van. On the Metro the devil kept saying, 'Get off the train and *go*!' But I didn't!

And what happened between Miguel and Loli? Miguel concludes the story:

As regards Loli, we began to have more peace about our relationship and the staff gave us permission to see each other again. They were quite favourable, in fact from the very beginning Raúl had said, 'Loli is for you. You're going to have to go your separate ways and grow spiritually and then come back together at some point.' That's what happened.

We were married on May 2nd, 1992, and we now have a little boy whose name is David.

As far as AIDS is concerned, I can talk about it. The devil didn't want us to get married. We were in a van and had a bad accident just a week before our wedding. I was given a test for AIDS and it came back positive.

I was really discouraged and had to talk to Loli. I said, 'I've got the virus; maybe we shouldn't get married.' I felt really condemned over this, but Loli said it didn't matter. She wanted to get married. We talked about it with the leaders, Elliott and Raúl. Since Raúl had had the same experience and had infected his own wife, he told me that he had faced a lot of condemnation.

He emphasized the hard truths and reality of a 'mixed' marriage and what it might mean for Loli and any children we might have. However, he also spoke of the will of God and the quality of life over mere length of life. In the end he left the decision to us. We decided to be married.

5

THE CHILDREN HAD TO GO
The story of Javier and Paqui Gonzalez

Here is an example of the ingenuity that addicts employ in order to survive. This young couple learnt the technique of fronting up at the local council office and asking for accommodation in the city 'refuge'. This would usually be granted for a few days, during which they would beg on the street until they had enough money for drink, drugs and the train fare to the next town.
We start with Javier.

The story of my battle with drugs commences when I was eighteen and working in photocomposition for a Madrid newspaper. There were periods of the day which were 'dead spots'; no news was coming in, and it was at one of these times that a female reporter suggested we go out and smoke a 'porro' (tobacco laced with hashish). Then a reporter who had been on assignment in Northern Europe brought back some LSD with which I also experimented.

I had a girlfriend called Paqui. We had a very intimate relationship and as a result she became pregnant. This upset me since we weren't married and I started to worry about her parents' reaction. As an escape from reality I went out more and more at night and tried other drugs, like amphetamines.

In order to pacify Paqui's family we decided to be married. This was in October, 1981 and by January of the next year I was due to join the military for national service.

Thanks to my newspaper job I had plenty of money and

was able to buy whatever I wanted. I knew the drug dealers on the street and so was able to buy heroin, which I began to sniff more and more, although at this time I wasn't mainlining.

When I joined the military I was sent to Zaragoza, 300 kilometres from Madrid, where I knew no one. I could not find heroin so I started to have withdrawal symptoms. I didn't know what these were and just thought I had the 'flu. I couldn't sleep and felt very sick. I became jittery and anxious but could not get out of the barracks.

I was there for only five days when Paqui gave birth to our son. I was given a few days leave and went back to Madrid. As soon as I had a fix I felt better and then realised I had been going through withdrawal.

Back in the army I made an application to be transferred back to Madrid for family reasons, but this seemed to be lost and was never processed, so I had to stay on in Zaragoza.

We were free in the evenings from five o'clock, so we used to go into town to drink or buy hashish. I didn't have enough money to buy heroin. I became very rebellious about military discipline. I hated the trumpet at reveille, and was constantly disobeying orders and being 'confined to barracks', so I was seldom able to go home to see my wife and son.

Paqui picks up the story:

I met Javi when I was sixteen, while working in a pharmacy. He joined our gang and it was when I was with these young people that I started to smoke hashish. I became pregnant at seventeen and, as Javi has said, we were married in 1981 and had our own apartment. After the birth of my son, Javier, I became pregnant again with our daughter, Irene.

When Javi came out of the military we badly wanted to

escape from the world of drugs, so we placed our son with my parents and our daughter with my sister. We then went off to Cercedilla, a retreat in Madrid run by some followers of Scientology. They helped us through the withdrawal period by having us take saunas; that sweated the poison out of our systems quickly. But after three months we left for home.

My parents now thought we were rehabilitated, so they gave us the care of their home while they went off on vacation. We took a lot of items from the house and sold them for drug money. When they returned we deceived them and told them we had given the things to friends because someone had threatened to rob the house, but they knew right away what we had done.

With two things in mind we decided to go to Santander. We knew of a Catholic priest who was taking in addicts, and if that did not work out we knew of a rehabilitation place called RETO.

We found the priest but we left as soon as we had gone through withdrawal. Dismissing the idea of RETO, we then went to the city refuge, a home for beggars and street people. It was here that we learned a new way to live and support ourselves.

The vagabonds at the refuge taught us that once we had stayed a while at one city refuge and done some begging, we could then buy a train ticket to the next city and do the same again. We did this for eight months. Every morning we started with a bottle of wine—that was our breakfast. We were not using drugs during that period because we could not afford to; we were more alcoholics than heroin addicts.

In our travels we met two gypsy youths who spoke to us about the 'Church of Philadelphia', a Pentecostal gypsy denomination; they took us to one of their churches and we joined in their singing and sensed that the people loved us.

This helped soften our attitude towards the gospel. Then we heard about Betel, but it had separate centres for men and women, so we had to split up when we went in.

Javi continues:

Paqui went to another WEC-related centre in Torrejón and I went to a farm run by Betel at Mejorada, outside of Madrid. I arrived on a Wednesday and that evening had to go to their regular meeting; I sat there watching and listening. Later I was put in a room with several other men and they talked quite a bit about the Bible.

During that first week they cut my hair, which was long, knotted and dirty. Soon after, I started to become aware of my filthiness, both internally and externally. Before, when I used to travel on the metro, people would move away from me because of my heavy odour, but here it did not seem to matter; they stuck with me and related closely to me.

For the first couple of weeks I worked at moving sand out of a large cistern. There was another fellow there but he left after a couple of days. This really depressed me, but two other men, who were my 'shadows', stayed with me and encouraged me.

I had stopped smoking when I arrived, but I started again and tried to conceal it. They caught me and as a result I had to wash dishes every night for a month. Someone said to me, 'Your difficulty is not having to do dishes, but why you were made to do them.' I realised then that my problem wasn't drugs or tobacco, but rather a rebellious heart.

Six weeks later I was sent to the centre at Cuenca and it was there that I started to have a hunger for God's fulness. I read the Gospels through a couple of times and became aware of the Holy Spirit. A group came to visit us from Colchester in England, and I remember Elliott and Mary, with Kent and Mary Alice and these English people, praying over me. The Lord really met me there.

At a worship service one day, the speaker told a story that spoke to my heart. A man bought a car but it broke down. He called in a mechanic, but shortly after it stopped again. After several more breakdowns he thought, 'The only thing I can do is to go back to the maker, who really understands it, and have it fixed properly.' That really touched me. I realised that I had been trying to 'jump-start' my life with various methods, but I had never gone to my Maker. This brought me to the Lord and I was born again. After a year and a half in Betel I was given a position of responsibility over quite a number of workers and tasks.

Paqui now continues her story from when she went into the centre at Torrejón:

Sandra, a WEC missionary from New Zealand, plus three other girls were there to receive me. I was just like a beggar. I was filthy and my hair was in knots. It touched me that they wanted to care for me, unlike the people outside, who used to keep away from me. Sandra was my 'shadow' and she stayed with me as I started to adjust to life at the centre. I was given the task of cleaning the house and, of course, had to attend the morning devotional meetings. I thought they were absurd, of no value whatsoever.

Shortly after passing through withdrawal I went out with another girl who was considered a 'responsible' person, but she had been there only three months. She asked me if I wanted a cigarette while we were out selling calendars. That led to my starting to smoke again.

One day a group from our residence was invited to another Betel branch, so fifteen of us went. Something touched me that day. Up till then I had no faith, but I was starting to ask questions. 'Is all this true?' Juan, now the Betel leader in Barcelona, gave his testimony, showing that Christ was really alive and doing miracles. (His changed life proved that.) The Lord really spoke to me.

The leader of our centre was called Tito. He shared the Bible with us regularly and told us that we were all precious in God's sight. That really touched me because I saw myself as simply worthless.

During the first couple of months there had been appeals at the end of meetings for people to accept Christ. I had put up my hand a number of times but I hadn't really meant it. The proof was in the packet of cigarettes I still kept in my pocket.

But eventually God's Spirit broke through. One of the leaders quoted a Bible verse: 'I will restore to you the years that the locust has eaten.' He urged us, 'Give thanks to God that he is restoring your life.' For the first time I was truly humbled and genuinely thankful. I had had many false starts at restoring my life, but finally I had reached the end of myself. I really repented and trusted the Lord.

Now we have our son, Javi (age 11), living with us, as well as our youngest daughter, one-year-old Ester. My sister has no children and wants to adopt our oldest daughter, Irene, who is nine. This is a great struggle for us. We understand the sacrifice my sister made to care for Irene when we were irresponsible addicts, and the strong emotional ties she and Irene have developed. We want the best for everyone. Nevertheless, we are believing a promise from the Lord that he will bring our child back. That will be another miracle.

Javi and Paqui are now ordained pastors and the leaders of the Betel centre and church in Cuenca.

6

CONQUESTS IN CUENCA -
CONSERVATIVE, CAUTIOUS AND CATHOLIC

Cuenca, about 180 kilometres east of Madrid, is a conservative and staunchly Catholic town. WEC has for many years targeted it as a needy area and successive missionaries have laboured there with only very limited success.

As the Betel work in Madrid grew, new converts were available to help with street witnessing, so it was agreed that teams should go there from time to time to help the resident missionaries in their church-planting efforts.

Miguel Jambrina, then leader, shares the story of the early days:

I remember one day we were helping WEC evangelise Cuenca. I knew that over the years many missionaries had been trying to establish a church, so we were going from house to house in one of the suburbs. I was placed with Jim Regan, a very new worker. He was from England. We also had Frank Stoorvogel from Holland, Wolfram Schumann from Germany, and Billy Glover from Ireland, plus a lady from some other country—it was like a meeting of the United Nations!

Jim didn't speak Spanish very well—he was so new. He would start to talk and then become tongue-tied. When he couldn't finish a conversation he'd motion to me and I'd have to speak for him. But I was brand new too. This was my first experience of witnessing. We did that all day and then went back to Madrid. From that time I had the burden of Cuenca on my heart.

Later, Elliott suggested that Juan Carlos and I go and establish a permanent work there.

I remember the first house we rented. It was on the Calle Santa Monica and it was a ruin, but we started working and fixed the whole place up. Finally we had it all painted inside but the day we finished there was a big rain storm. The roof wasn't good and the plaster fell down. We were very discouraged when we saw that everything was stained. But we went back to work and fixed it up again.

We did a lot of evangelising, going from door to door with Frank Stoorvogel and Juan Torres, a Spaniard who had married an Australian missionary and had joined WEC. But there was little fruit.

In October, 1988 the first jobs we were asked to do were painting and brickwork. We also started a small second-hand furniture shop but that did not do too well. However, bit by bit, people became more acquainted with us.

There was one major difference—there weren't many addicts. Our community had some from Cuenca but most were sent to us by other Betel centres that were over-crowded. Actually, the Cuenca church has been built on the families of just a few addicts. Even though they were few in number, they were sufficient to give us a start.

Betel helped three of the worst addicts in Cuenca. The first was Carmen, who is now the wife of the Betel pastor in charge of the work in Barcelona. She was the worst case. She had an awful reputation in the town and was very sickly; when the team first met her, she was in bad shape. Now she is a beautiful transformed woman, mature, able to counsel people, dignified. One would never recognise her as having been an addict. And of course her family—her mother and father and some other members—have been converted and become part of the church.

The second was Lourdes. She later died of AIDS, but not before she heard the gospel. She had a very sad life, even going out on the streets as a prostitute at one time. She had a problem with gangrene that resulted in her having a part of her hand amputated.

Then there was Juan. He is not really right with God now, but the team picked him off the street and tried to help him, then he had to go back to prison to serve a sentence for an earlier crime. But his mother became a Christian and is now a baptised member of the church.

While the men were still living in the Santa Monica building there was an alarming incident which Elliott describes:

We had an Iranian fellow with us by the name of Ressa. He was an architect who had been a heroin addict but had been cured at Betel. Early one morning, in the third floor attic where we had the devotionals, he was trying to light our wood-burning stove. The wood was hard to ignite so he foolishly took a five litre can of gasoline and started to pour it on to what he thought were dead coals. But they were still hot from the night before and the whole thing exploded knocking over the can of gasoline which also caught fire. The whole house was filled with smoke. Everybody panicked and ran outside. Alfredo and Ressa had the presence of mind to soak blankets with water and tried to put the fire out.

A long wooden roof covered the whole terrace of houses of which ours was one, so the fire had the potential of running the whole length of the building and destroying the entire block. The two men, battling smoke inhalation, continued to douse the flames and eventually these died down, partly because there were no windows to admit fresh air.

We found later that the wood in the attic had started to

burn and turn to charcoal. The heat melted the TV; in fact it melted anything that was plastic. It turned the whole house black, but God again had, mercifully, spared us by smothering the fire in an enclosed area. If it had continued the whole block of houses would have gone up in flames and we would have been disgraced. We repaired the house and carried on as if nothing had happened.

Eventually we transferred the men from Calle Santa Monica to Mariana, a beautiful picturesque village ten kilometres out of Cuenca. We were all ready to start there in a beautiful small hotel, but the local people, once they knew who we were, began to persecute us. They didn't understand how a drug centre worked. They thought we were coming with drugs, syringes, diseases and problems, so they rejected us. In a small open yard, fifty neighbours came together and began to throw stones at the house. Then they started shouting insults at us, demanding that we leave and telling us that if we didn't they would burn the house down during the night.

They demanded that the leader go to the city council, so Miguel went to talk to the mayor. Why did they want to kick the group out? What wrong had been committed? The people mobbed the leaders and pushed them violently out of the council chambers.

Miguel called Madrid, and I decided to go immediately and support him. We both went again to the council building. A mob of about one hundred turned up, shouting and screaming. The air was as full of cigarette smoke as it was of confusion. We tried to reason with them but they insisted we had to leave. No ifs or buts about it. They did not want us there. We had no permission and no licence, we had to go or they would denounce us to the Guardia Civil (National Police). We listened to them politely and tried to explain rationally what our programme was like, that we weren't

136

drug addicts, that we were seeking to cure addicts, that we didn't even smoke or drink. But our words fell on deaf ears. They insisted we must leave. I said, 'No'; we were standing on our rights and not moving. We had as much right to live in Mariana as anyone else. We had a rental contract and we were going to occupy the house. And furthermore, we were within all the ordinances and limits of the law.

After a month or two we began to send more people by ones and twos, until we unobtrusively filled the house. Living in the village, we let them see what we were like. All the while they were observing us. We would walk through the streets and say 'good morning', 'good afternoon', 'good day' and the people wouldn't even talk to us. But bit by bit things began to change. Today the situation has been totally reversed. They are now our friends and I think I can say without exaggeration that they actually love us. They have given us lots of work. In fact, we have probably painted the whole pueblo—almost every house in the village. They used to have to call painters from Cuenca; now when the people want their house painted they knock on our door and say, 'Could you please come down and paint our house?'

About a year after they stoned us, they published in their small local paper (a hand-typed, photocopied newspaper) an article, publicly asking forgiveness for their bad attitude and their mistreatment of us. Now they come down to our house and visit us just like they would visit any other family in the pueblo. The women have coffee with us; the men talk about sports and farming—we are part of the village.

Mariana is now a kind of paradise for us. Betel men can take a walk in the streets and everyone stops to talk to them and befriend them. They are continually showering us with gifts. Each year the city council donates all the firewood we need for the winter.

Miguel kept searching for a better place for the girls and eventually after two years found an empty barn that had been used for raising pigs. It was made of cinder block but it had no floor, windows or plumbing and was unpainted.

Elliott tells what happened:

We really didn't want a barn, we needed a house, nevertheless we decided to go and look at it. We saw that it was spacious and that it had plenty of land around it, so in view of our desperate need we decided to make an offer of five million pesetas, one million down and four million over four years. (A million pesetas was then worth between $8,000-9,000.) The owner accepted, so we started the big task of remodelling it.

At that time we did not have any good builders, not even a bricklayer; we had no electricians or plumbers, but still we decided to go ahead. One man said although he didn't have a lot of experience at bricklaying he would try. We managed to build several internal walls to ceiling height but had no ceiling—just the roof. I called Tito in Almería and found he had a plasterer, so he came and quickly fixed a beautiful ceiling over these divisions. Then we put tiles on the walls, and within three months the transformation was complete.

But the team was desperate for a really good practical man and it was then that they thought of Manolito. Here is his story from the person who had first contact with him—Sue Regan, a WEC missionary from Britain.

Manolito came from Madrid. His mother died when he was young and, as his father was not able to control him, he sent him away to a reformatory. He was a troublemaker and suffered hard treatment at the hands of his teachers.

One day he was beaten and ended up with a nasty gash

on his head. He escaped and found his way back to Madrid. No one wanted him, but an uncle said he could live with him if he helped him in his bakery. So at the age of twelve he had to rise early and help in the bake house instead of going to school. If he fell asleep, his uncle would beat him.

Once again he decided that he had had enough physical abuse, so he ran away and started life 'on the street'. He fell as far as he could fall—drinking, robbery, drugs and so on, always looking for something to fill the aching void inside, and never finding it.

One of the many tragic episodes during his drug-crazed years had very serious repercussions. One night he was robbing a shop. He had obtained the use of a big truck and he and a companion were loading the stolen goods on to it. The neighbours realised what was happening and called the police. Two police cars came and blocked each end of the street. The two men saw only one car. So Manolito quickly started the truck and headed for the other end of the street. Then they saw the second car so he suddenly went into reverse. He did not know that the first car was now pursuing them, so backed the truck right into it, decapitating both policemen. When he discovered what he had done he almost lost his mind. In fact he was put in a mental hospital for a long while, and then had to go to prison for four years.

However, after all that he went back to a life of drug addiction. He and a friend 'happened' to pass through Tarancón, where we lived, one Saturday afternoon. They went to the Town Hall to beg for money. The mayor gave them our address, so they came to our building and buzzed our apartment. I went to the front door thinking they were ex-drug addicts from Betel whom we were expecting for a meeting in our church that night. But when I saw them I realised my mistake—they were obviously living rough and suffering from the effects of drugs.

139

As we learned later, when we asked them in, they thought we were an easy 'touch' and were thinking of robbing us. We gave them a meal and invited them to the meeting which they attended, both obviously going through the symptoms of withdrawal.

Through that contact Manolito went back to Madrid and finally found at Betel what he had been craving for all these years—a loving, caring community and a heavenly Father's love which would never fail.

Elliott concludes:

Miguel, the leader in Cuenca, decided he would invite Manolito to join the work. It would be true to say that he really met the Lord in a new way there, and was probably converted at that time. His life changed radically. He was a very good mechanic and handy at any kind of practical work. He could carry on in extremely cold weather, getting down under vans and cars in freezing temperatures. He became a real servant, and would tackle any job even though he was suffering from AIDS.

He went on very well, but then fell in love with Elo, one of our girls. We approved of their relationship because by this time they were both mature leaders.

But suddenly she broke it off and told him she didn't want to see him any more. Within two weeks he died of AIDS. I believe he died of a broken heart—there was no physical reason for this sudden downturn in his health.

This shows us the direct relationship between a person's attitude and physical well-being. If he had wanted to live he could have lived; medical authorities confirm that. Dr. Buzon, the founder and director of Madrid's first AIDS clinic, has noted, in dealing with our fellows, that they have a hope that affects their physical condition. Consequently they live longer than the average AIDS patient. Grace, holiness, hope and even simple determination continue to extend their lives.

Manolito had a tremendous impact on other lives during the few years he walked with God. All our present leaders have been deeply influenced by him. For some reason they all loved him more than almost anybody else.

We were in the Canary Islands when I heard about Elo breaking off the relationship and the effect this had on him, so I immediately wrote him a letter to console him and to assure him that God had someone better. I urged him to stand firm in the Lord. But he died before it reached him.

Today there is a thriving church in Cuenca, meeting in an excellent downtown property. Ex-addicts and their families constitute the backbone of the congregation. WEC missionaries, Juan and Barbara Torres, have had a strong pastoral ministry there, but have now moved on leaving Javi and Paqui as the new pastors.

7

FROM CRIME TO CHRIST
The Story of Tomás and Trini

We begin Tomás' story when he was eighteen and living in the town of Tarancón, 100 kilometres from Madrid. By that age he was taking LSD habitually. An annual festival was going on in the village of Saelices, so, with three other lads (two sixteen-year-olds and another of his own age) he decided to go; they were all euphoric on LSD.

They didn't have transport, so they decided to steal a car, and found one in a quiet street late at night. They forced open the door and one of them fixed the ignition leads so it would start. Before turning on the engine they pushed it away from where it was parked. Then they hit a problem— the steering lock was still in position. They kicked the steering wheel till the lock broke and drove off. One of the sixteen-year-old lads was driving and Tomás was in the back seat.

Suddenly the steering lock mechanism fell into place again, and with the front wheels fixed they drove straight through the plate-glass window of a tractor company show-room.

The two older fellows threatened the younger ones with dire retribution if they told anyone about them, and then disappeared. No one saw these two leave, but the two younger ones were seen by a neighbour who reported them to the police. They were eventually caught but didn't divulge the others' names, so their parents had to make good the damage.

The sequel to this event comes some time later, when Tomás entered Betel in Madrid. He kept hearing references

to a Spanish missionary, Juan Torres, who was working
with WEC, and had his car stolen in Tarancón. The more
details he heard, the more convinced he was that this was
the car he and his companions had stolen. Tomás recalls:

When I realised this, I immediately shut up. I didn't say a
word to anybody for four or five months until I came to
Christ and was born again. Not long after this I was sitting
up one night with a new arrival who was going through
withdrawal. The leader of the house, Raúl Casto, came in
quite late, around eleven o'clock, and we started to talk.
Somehow the story of the missionary's stolen car came up
and I couldn't stand it any longer; I blurted out the whole
story. Raúl said that I had an obligation to go to Juan Torres
and ask his forgiveness.

Time passed and Tomás was asked to help at a new
rehabilitation centre started by other members of WEC in
connection with the church at Concepción. One day a
visiting speaker arrived at the service and it was none other
than the man he dreaded to meet—Juan Torres! By now
Tomás was one of the leaders in this fellowship, so it was a
big thing for him to go to Juan and confess. He went up to
him and said, 'Juan, even though I was never found out, I
was one of the fellows who stole your car in Tarancón.'

Juan's reaction was, 'Listen, if this has served the
purpose of bringing you to know Jesus, then let's just praise
God for it.' Juan went on to tell him that since that night the
missionaries had prayed for the culprits that they would one
day be converted. Tomás firmly believed that God worked
in his life in answer to those prayers.

Australian missionaries Lindsay and Myk McKenzie re-
turned from home leave. Before going to Australia they had

handed their responsibilities in Madrid over to others, so on return they were ready for a fresh start elsewhere, and the Betel team felt that they should pioneer a new work in Valencia. Myk and Lindsay's choice for a Spanish leader was Tomás, so they asked him over to have a meal with them in their flat and put the proposition to him. As he was not deeply involved in anything in Madrid he readily agreed to go.

After Tomás had served for six months as leader of the men's house in Valencia, Trini arrived with a group of girls to head up a new residence for women. Tomás takes up the story:

I knew Trini from the days when we were both students at the Adullam Bible School run by Betel. I have to admit I wasn't attracted to her then, but in Valencia, because of our leadership responsibilities, we had to deal with each other often on a work basis. It was a platonic friendship at first, then it started to develop into something more. Something was happening between us, but at the same time I didn't want to rush ahead. I wanted God to confirm it to me before I made any direct moves. I was enjoying my work and I knew that marriage would mean I would have to leave direct contact with the centre, and I wasn't ready for that. One day I went with Lindsay to the local prison and as we came out he stopped me. 'Is there anything between you and Trini?' My reply was, 'Well, no, there's nothing, but from my point of view, yes, there's an interest.' Lindsay at that moment encouraged me to go ahead.

It took me three months to come round to deciding to approach her. On many occasions I tried to open up the subject, but as soon as I was close to her I had cold feet and talked about something else. One particular Sunday morning the sermon was on faith, and I thought, 'This is it. This is the moment to act.' I had to talk to Trini about some financial matter to do with the centre, so after the service, while people were leaving, I asked her to accompany me downstairs to the shop and there, amongst all the second-hand furniture I said, 'There are two things I need to talk to you about. Firstly, do you have the tithes from the girls' work? And secondly, God has told me to marry you.' Her immediate reply was, 'What am I supposed to do?' I said, 'I expect you to say "yes".' She told me it was so sudden; she didn't know what to do. I told her she didn't have to say anything at that moment, but two days later she told me 'Yes'. There was a six month engagement period and then we were married.

It was actually during their honeymoon on the Canary Islands that the idea of serving God somewhere in the Mediterranean area arose. One day Trini said, 'I could live here forever. This is a beautiful island.' Tomás replied, 'I would have a problem if God called me to an island; I feel so isolated and shut in.' This incident passed, but it was followed by another when they were passing through Madrid en route to Valencia again. Several leaders there expressed the thought that it was time for Betel to commence a work in Majorca. Trini and Tomás both warmed to that idea. A further confirmation came when Lindsay called them from Valencia and asked them to consider heading a new advance there as an extension of the Valencia work.

But meanwhile they still had to prove themselves in the work as a married couple, so they returned to Valencia, where, as Trini shares in her testimony, they were not without their problems.

First, however, we will let her tell the story of her early life:

145

I came from a working class family and my father drank a lot, but even though he had this problem, he was a dutiful father and husband. He was a hard worker, and he provided for the family. We lived in a farmhouse on the outskirts of a town called Arganda Del Rey. One factor that influenced the way I behaved was that, living a fair way from the city, we had to leave for school very early on a bus, returning very late at night. Nobody knew what I did in between those times.

When I was twelve or thirteen, this free time was what led me to experiment with my friends. I would steal regularly from my mother, taking money from her purse without her knowing. It became a habit I took as a right. When I was young, my friends were a lot older so I had this desire to do 'older' things. At fourteen I began to smoke, and in no time I was taking joints—tobacco laced with hashish. Then it wasn't long before I started taking amphetamines. On week days I would smoke hashish and at weekends I would take amphetamines and LSD.

During this time I wasn't working, of course. I bought all these drugs with money I'd stolen from my parents. My father would receive his wage every two weeks and no-one would imagine that someone from the family would steal; the money was always kept in a metal box in the lounge room and every two weeks, when my father would get his pay cheque, I would take out 5,000 pesetas.

At sixteen I was expelled from school for stealing money, so I found employment at a slaughter house. My job was to wash the intestines of the animals that were killed; they later made sausage skins out of them. It wasn't very pleasant but I earned a lot of money. I had a basic wage for working from seven till three, but what my family didn't know was that I would do overtime and that money I would keep for myself. I would hand the basic wage to my parents (which is what is usually done in Spain).

Little by little I advanced from soft drugs to heroin. Then, as heroin became a necessity my character began to change. I became disagreeable with my friends and I even began to hate myself. What was happening revolted me but I was powerless to do anything about it. The craving for heroin intensified, and if I didn't take it I would start to go through withdrawal pains that were unpleasant. In order to get through a day I would first go into the toilet at work and have a fix.

The plan to steal the payroll

My average monthly wage was usually between $700-1000—more than what others of my age were earning. In spite of having this I needed more to pay for my ever-increasing doses of heroin.

About 100 people were employed at the meat works and we were paid in cash on the same day each month. I tried to work out a way to steal the payroll. There was only one obstacle; a security guard was employed on each shift. One of these knew me personally, so I had to organise the robbery when he was not on duty. The office was on the third floor of the complex and the people were all working downstairs, so if I had to steal this money I would have to go there without anybody seeing me. That was almost impossible.

So I finally figured out that if I presented my plan to two friends who weren't employees there—if I gave them all the details of where the money was and how to get there—we could do it and reap the benefits. So these two friends went at night but they couldn't open the strong box. In the end they found 50,000 pesetas ($500) in another drawer, but people came up the stairs to see what was going on, so they ran away and left the payroll intact.

Rumours started going around that I was involved with drugs, and some people even began to ask me if I knew anything about the robbery. So when my two years contract was up they didn't renew it. The firm gave me a rather large severance payment which I spent on drugs. Within ten days it was all gone, spent not just on myself, but on my friends. I told my parents that they hadn't given me anything.

I began to live more and more apart from my family. I wouldn't give them explanations of where I'd been or what I was doing. I had contacts with men whom I knew would give me money for sleeping with them. Whenever I needed cash for heroin I would ring one and I'd be sure of getting some money. That was one form of income. The other was simply to go to my parents and rob whatever I could. I remember once I took all of my father's monthly wage. The final straw for my family was when I went to the bank and forged my father's signature to take money out of his account.

We now shift our focus from Trini herself to a Spanish lady whom God, in his sovereign purpose, used to steer her on to the path of life. This account has been written by Myk McKenzie.

Pepi ran a small shop next to a bar where young drug addicts gathered to drink and hang out. Pepi was a Christian, and a praying woman. Day by day her burden for her noisy neighbours grew. Some days after she locked up, she would get down on her knees inside her shop and intercede for the young people. She was particularly burdened for one young girl who looked and acted more like a man.

One evening after she closed up the shop she found her propped up against the shop window and said, 'Hi, I feel I almost know you. What's your name?'

'My name's Trini,' she replied.

From then on, whenever Pepi saw the opportunity, she greeted Trini and often gave her fresh fruit, a nourishing yoghurt or a home-made biscuit. And she prayed all the harder, asking God to do a miracle in the girl's life.

One day Pepi ventured, 'You need to go to a place where they'll care for you and help free you from heroin.' But Trini wouldn't listen and insisted that she wasn't an addict.

A week or so later Trini came banging on Pepi's door, while she was on her knees praying, and desperately asked for help. She had an address of a center in Madrid and only wanted the bus fare. Pepi gave Trini the money and thanked God for answering her prayer. She even laughed and cried and danced around her shop after Trini left.

But the next morning, when the shop door opened, there was Trini in the doorway. In dismay Pepi exclaimed, 'Trini, what are you doing here?'

'I'm sorry, but I used the money to shoot-up. Please give me another chance! I'm really desperate!'

Pepi sighed, but her mother's heart was moved with compassion and she opened the till and handed Trini her second bus fare to Madrid.

The very same day as Pepi was closing up the shop she glanced to her left and then dropped her keys in shock. There was Trini, propped up against the shop window again.

Indignation and bewilderment filled Pepi's heart. 'Why did you do it?' she burst out. 'You know I won't give you money to shoot up. That's it! I've had enough.' But she saw the look of panic in Trini's face.

'Pepi, don't abandon me! Please, I am dying. Just one more chance. Believe me.'

Again compassion flooded Pepi's heart. She reached into her handbag and gave Trini the fare. 'Don't ask me again, Trini,' she warned, 'this is the last time.' And it was.

As the bus sped on its way to Madrid, Trini's mind was in a whirl. She thought she was crazy and she remembered that they had told her in the hospital that her days were numbered! So why bother?

But she remembered Pepi's encouragement and her mother's pleas while she had been in the hospital—and a voice, one she'd only heard when around Pepi, 'Don't give up.'

'Yes, I've got to keep going,' she told herself again.

It seemed an eternity before the vehicle pulled into the busy terminal. She headed in the direction of the taxis. The first driver refused to take her, as did the second and the third all the way down the line of taxis. The same scene, the same rejection.

She went into a bar for a drink, then returned and started down the line again until she came to the last taxi.

'Look mister, I've only got 700 pesetas to my name, but I'm a junkie and I've got to get help.' She took the crumpled paper with the address and waved it in his face. 'Can you take me to this place? They help people like me. I've got to get there!'

The cab driver looked at his street directory and even though it meant crossing the city said, 'Get in.'

They eventually pulled up beside a door and a huge white wall with the words *Centro Betel* in bold blue.

Before she got out she leaned over and said, 'I'll never forget what you've done for me,' and handed him the 700 pesetas.

'Forget it,' he replied, 'Just get cured.'

Help at last
Trini looked for a bell or doorknocker, but finding neither knocked on the large double doors before her. No one answered. She tried again, this time loudly. A neighbour on the third floor stepped out on her balcony and called across the street to a young man on Betel's second storey balcony.

'Hey! Someone's at your door!' He walked down the stairs and opened the door and asked Trini what he could do.

'I'm here to be admitted,' she retorted.

Armando replied, 'Sorry, but it's Saturday evening and we close for the weekend. Come back on Monday.'

'What! I can't come back another day! I am not moving until you let me in, even if I have to stay all weekend!'

Armando paused to think. 'Follow me,' he said, and led her the half kilometre to the Teppers' house. Elliott opened the door and let the two in. Armando explained the situation, and although it was the weekend they both agreed to make an exception and drive her out to the women's residence in Torrejón. Elliott gave him the keys to his car and then Armando, the Teppers' son, Jonathan, and Trini made the twenty minute trip to Torrejón.

Trini did not remember much of the trip to the women's house, but she did remember being received by a kindly Mexican woman named Teresa. Her belongings were searched. Then she was coaxed into a shower and given a clean, warm tracksuit. Finally she fell on to a sofa and at last gave in to the overwhelming waves of exhaustion. It wasn't until Tuesday afternoon that she felt fit enough to sit up and eat. Then slowly Trini fell into the routine of the Betel Community's lifestyle.

At the end of a month the leaders of the house, Sarah and Carmen, felt that she was ready to work with the other girls in the street. She responded to the loving care of the Betel family, and light began to penetrate her understanding as she participated in morning devotions and attended the Friday night and Sunday morning public meetings. She was amazed at the relevance of Bible truth.

Trini had her struggles with herself, community discipline and tobacco, but she found that the Betel people loved her in spite of her struggles.

Trini now continues the story in her own words.

Their friendship and concern were fantastic, and they didn't ask for anything in exchange. Never in my life—not even in my own family—had I experienced this kind of selfless love. And yet, at the same time, I felt empty. I was now doing everything right externally, but inside there was still an aching void. One day things came to a head. I was on my own, and was feeling so depressed that I just broke down and cried. I wasn't a person to do that easily. I couldn't remember the last time I had cried. 'God, please help me,' I said. I went to Carmen again and shared with her what had happened. She helped me to understand the forgiveness of God. Since then, I've had an inner strength and peace that I've never known before. With Carmen's careful discipling I have kept my eyes focused on Jesus.

After six months I asked to be baptised. I didn't fully understand what it meant but I knew that it was a step of obedience and that God would bless me for obeying him. I must confess that I even thought baptism was a kind of 'magic wand' and I'd be transformed into a saint, so it was a great shock to realise afterwards that it wasn't like that.

In all this period of struggle I was growing, and the leaders were teaching me that while it's one thing to be in the centre receiving help, it's another to give to others and start concentrating on their problems. It was then that it was proposed that I take on the responsibility of a second-hand furniture shop. For me it was an incredible thing that they should want to give me that responsibility, and I really took it seriously. It was a personal challenge which I enjoyed and I wanted to make it a financial success. We had good sales and I enjoyed that experience. About eleven months after starting at Betel I was ready for more responsibility and the leaders proposed that I go to Valencia. I agreed to this.

Tomás relates in his testimony how God led us together, so I'll go on to describe what happened after we were married.

I started into marriage thinking that all the problems I'd had as a single person were now behind me and I would have no more struggle in certain areas. But that idea simply gave the devil an entrance and before long I fell.

One night I went out with one of the girls who used to be in the centre, and took heroin. Having failed once, I went out a second time and tried to drown my sorrows with alcohol. I was totally shocked when I realised afterwards what I had done. My actions not only caused pain in my heart, but they had involved another person. They had also caused great grief and suffering to my husband. The final realisation was that I had tried to deceive the Lord. I went into a deep depression and didn't even want to live any more. Every day the horror of what I had done swept over me and I couldn't face the future.

It even crossed my mind that I should drop Christianity, leave the work, and toss everything overboard. The only thing that kept me going was the patience, love and supportiveness of Tomás.

Elliott Tepper describes subsequent events:

Discipline, of course, had to be imposed on Trini. We transferred them both back to Madrid where they were placed in a community of other married people. Tomás was not removed from leadership, but his role was changed. Being in Madrid he was kept on the leaders' council and attended the pastors' meeting, whereas Trini was excluded from that for six months. But what ministered to them more than anything else was the love and the acceptance that they received and the forgiveness shown to them. They were surrounded by a loving family, and folk just accepted them in spite of what had happened.

Trini concludes:

The time came when our return to Valencia was to be discussed. It made me nervous because I knew coming back would be difficult. Everybody there knew what had happened. (In Madrid some people knew a few of the details but it wasn't generally known.) When we returned I had this fear that maybe people would remember and maybe throw it in my face ... I feared, for example, going to give a devotional in the girls' house; perhaps they would think: 'Look who's talking! How can you say that after what's happened to you?' But I haven't experienced any kind of rejection at all, rather the opposite. I feel people's forgiveness and acceptance. There are no barriers, there's complete healing, I believe.

Going to Majorca excites me in many ways—not just the fact of leaving here and starting somewhere else; it's the fact that God is willing to trust me again and he wants to use me. I'm still useful to him, in spite of everything.

Tomás and Trini were sent to start the new Betel outreach in Majorca. Almost from the first, Trini's health began to fail. Trini passed into the presence of the Lord in July, 1994 after a brave struggle with AIDS. Tomás continues as the Betel pastor of the Majorca church and community.

8

FAITHFUL WIFE, FOOLISH HUSBAND
The story of Alicia and Augustín

Alicia was a surprise baby, born eight years after the last of the other four children, when her mother was already forty. So in one sense she was a lonely girl in her childhood years. The resultant strong desire for love and friendship found expression in her early teens when she began to flirt with boys. The peer value system said that if you didn't have a boyfriend by fourteen you were way behind the others. And if you hadn't been to bed with someone by sixteen then you were a nobody. Alicia describes her situation:

The pressure to succumb was so great that when, at seventeen, I met the young man who was to be my husband, I gave in, and soon was pregnant.

But from the moment I met Augustín my life was revolutionised: I started to discover the world of drugs—something totally unknown to me till then. At first there seemed nothing wrong in experimenting. It was fun, and nothing seemed to happen to us.

But then he was introduced to heroin. I'll never forget the first time he shot up in front of me. I was staggered at the change in his personality. He never suggested I take it, but as time went on I became annoyed because he just seemed to grab every opportunity to shoot up. Hashish wasn't enough; it had to be heroin, and, if possible, alcohol. Finally I had to tell him to stop. He realised he was becoming hooked, so by the time we were married he had stopped taking all drugs.

The first two years of their married life were reasonably good. They set up home in Torrejón, a suburb of Madrid, where they knew no one, so Augustín was removed from his old acquaintances, but little by little he started to gain new contacts in the drug world, and the day came when Alicia realised he was thoroughly hooked.

Alicia describes what followed:

Life became a slow, long hell. Augustín's dependency on heroin led him into a life of crime—breaking into properties and into vehicles. Twice he was sent to prison for two months at a time. These were terrible times. I had to keep house, care for the child and find work in order to survive financially.

Alicia, who had never become addicted, had a growing revulsion against her husband's way of life—a revulsion that turned into a hatred of him. There seemed to be only one way out—separation. She tried this, but in her wretched loneliness returned to him after six months. But she soon realised that normal living was an unreachable dream, as he pursued his drug-ridden way of life.

She takes up the story:

The neighbours who lived below us were Christians—ex-drug addicts, in fact, rehabilitated at Betel. They too had two daughters. I couldn't believe that they had been drug addicts, because there was nothing in their lifestyle that gave the slightest indication of their previous state. Their personal testimonies were fantastic. What most impressed me was the fact that they insisted that it was only the love of God that had been able to change their lives. I began to be quite friendly with them, especially with Marimar, the wife. There were so many things that amazed me about them—especially the fact that they didn't smoke and they didn't drink, even though they lived in front of a bar. They seemed so united as a couple. You could see that there was love in their home.

I'll never forget what happened when Augustín was back in prison again. By then I had had my second daughter, and there was no way I could work and pay the rent. I was told that we would have to vacate the flat. I had nowhere to go!

Marimar and Carlos came to my rescue. They talked to the leaders of Betel and asked if they could accept me and my two girls; they agreed, and so we moved in, even though I was not a drug addict needing rehabilitation.

When Augustín was released he was very angry with me and said it was my duty to come home and look after him, but I said it was no life being with him, and there could be no marriage in the true sense until he was off all drugs. So I refused to leave the centre. He used to arrive at the door of the women's residence and become very violent. On several occasions we had to call the police to remove him. The children saw all these horrible scenes and that has produced a complex in them that still exists today.

Things became so bad that the leaders of Betel in Madrid contacted the other centre in Valencia and asked the staff to take Alicia and the children. Valencia was under great pressure at the time. There were no spare rooms—only one huge dormitory full of women, but with the realisation that Augustín might one day turn up with a weapon and kill Alicia, the Valencia team agreed to her going to them.

Lindsay and Myk McKenzie take up the story:

We took them in and God gave us a deep love for Alicia and the children. It took a while for Alicia to assert control over

157

the children. Others were quick to do it because she was so laid back! But she made great strides; she's been with us for three years and we've never heard her complain.

Augustín entered four Betel centres at different times. At each place he simply walked out an angry man.

Augustín was released from prison in February 1994 under article 60 of the Penal Code which deals with 'release from prison because of terminal illness'. He joined his wife and children, but sadly died of AIDS in June. He had finally given his life to Jesus.

Eternity will know the greatness of Alicia's patience and long-suffering love towards her husband.

9

YOU MURDERED MY DAUGHTER
The story of Alfredo Tebá

Envy was Alfredo's downfall, right from childhood years when, living near an American Air Force base, he would see the children of airmen with their new bicycles and skateboards, and their parents driving around in the latest model cars. In contrast there he was, living in one bedroom with four other brothers and sisters! He says:

I was so envious of these children. I would regularly steal their toys. It was all so easy—I enjoyed the challenge of stealing. I didn't stop with them, I would steal from our neighbours, even my school teacher. My parents would beat me when they found out, but that didn't stop me; it had become an ingrained habit.

Through teenage years Alfredo continued in the same way, regularly being caught and jailed for short periods.
He became a welder but the long hours and meagre pay only heightened his compulsion to get rich by any way he could. He remembers one incident.

With two others I decided to rob a security firm that delivered payrolls. We bound all the employees, but we had neglected to tie the feet of one man. He rushed to a window and yelled into the street. Someone called the police and they arrived in time to catch us as we were escaping. I served six years in prison for that.

During these long years in prison there was plenty of time to reflect on his life. He had such a desire to be different but didn't know how; but one day a group of Christians came to witness, perform drama and share the gospel.

Alfredo recalls that event.

Their presentation brought tears to my eyes, but of course I didn't want other prisoners to see me. One of the team made his way over to me and told me that God loved me and could change my life. In my heart, that was exactly what I wanted! I sensed God was speaking to me then. The young man wanted to pray for me, but I wouldn't let him because I was embarrassed with other prisoners nearby. Anyway he assured me that he and the team would keep praying for me.

I knew that God had spoken directly to me through that group, but, mistakenly, I figured that a change would only come if I was married, had children and was thus compelled to act responsibly. I can remember praying that night that God would give me a wife (a *young* wife) and a child.

After prison Alfredo returned to his home in Alcalá de Guadaira, near Seville. Some local friends helped him to set up a small shoe repair business and this went quite well. It was also through these friends that he met María del Mar. Because his home was an unhappy place he decided to live on his own, and María would come round to make meals for him. The friendship developed and soon they were married.

But his old enemies, greed and envy, came back to haunt him again. He saw drug dealers making millions of pesetas, while he was working long hours for a modest income to support his wife and his new born son. Alfredo describes the temptation.

The dealers came to me and said, 'Hey, you don't take

heroin; you'd be a great pusher (trafficker), because there is no risk of your consuming it. You'd be making a lot more than you're making here. You think about it and we'll sell it to you. We'll trust you. You just say when.' I said 'no' because I knew if I started playing around with anything like that I'd end up being like them. Over the next few days and weeks I thought, 'I could be having a hundred thousand pesetas a day to spend on anything I wanted.' In the end I went to them and said, 'Give me some; I will try and sell it.'

After dealing where we lived we decided to go to Majorca. We sold the flat we were buying and went with 200,000 pesetas in cash and forty grams of heroin. (One gram cost $185 then.) The money lasted quite a while so we didn't worry about trying to sell the heroin. Instead we started taking it ourselves, in fact we used up 85% of it.

I managed to find work washing dishes in a restaurant but lasted only three days because the heroin had made me a physical wreck. We were flung out of the cheap hostel where we were living and went to a free one provided for vagrants by the city council. We were evicted from that as well, and ended up selling Kleenex tissues to motorists at traffic lights. We would take our son along to touch people's hearts.

We were reduced to sleeping in abandoned houses— until the police came along and threw us out. We found a caravan that had been in an accident and made that our home, but someone must have reported us to social welfare out of concern for little Oscar. Two officers from that department arrived one day just as we were shooting up. They removed the child and took him to a state refuge.

The immediate problem in Majorca was solved by María's mother coming over from the mainland. She obtained custody of little Oscar but before returning to Seville she visited Alfredo and María and gave them some money.

The authorities held them for a few days and then released them on the condition that they left Majorca immediately. They caught the first ferry to Valencia where they found accommodation in a cheap hostel.

During these early days in Valencia they had a strange encounter. A middle-aged respectable type of lady came up to María. Flora didn't say much, just 'God knows about your problem and loves you.' She then handed them a card with the name and address of a Christian rehabilitation centre on it. Alfredo slipped it into his shirt pocket and promptly forgot about it.

How were they to live? They decided to steal a motorbike and go in for bag-snatching. The person in front controls the cycle and the one on the back seat reaches out and grabs the handbag of a pedestrian as they go by. But things became worse when they had no more strength to go out and steal.

Alfredo continues:

We were so desperate that I even allowed María to prostitute herself so that we could have money for heroin. We had lost all sense of morality and decency. But I did not feel anything any more; all I wanted was heroin.

María's health began to suffer and I finally convinced her, much against her will, to go to hospital. The upper part of one of her arms had swollen to twice its normal size as a result of infection from a dirty syringe. She was diagnosed as having acute phlebitis.

Within twelve days she died. It seemed like a nightmare that could not possibly be true—a horror movie that would end soon and everything would be fine. But it didn't happen like that. María was only twenty-one.

I left the hospital and just walked and walked, not knowing where I was going. Finally I headed for the only place where I knew I could find relief—the suburb of La Malvarrosa and the first drug dealer I could find. I injected myself with a larger than normal dose, hoping that I would never wake up again. I must have lain for some hours in an open field and then gradually returned to consciousness.

Then I remembered the slip of paper that lady had given me days before. I thought of what she had said about God and decided to look for a church, thinking I might find him there.

I found one and went in. I saw a lady putting money into little boxes. Each time a coin went in the candles lit up. Then I saw a priest glaring at me. I said to myself, 'I don't think I'm going to find God here,' and left.

I looked at the address on the card I had been given. It said BETEL, so I made my way across the city to the address given. At reception I was told I needed to obtain a blood analysis before I could enter.

I went to the hospital to have the analysis and they told me to return for the report the next day. I slept in a truck that night and next day begged the hospital people to give me the report right away. They did so and I went over to be admitted at Betel.

What drew my attention was the treatment they gave me. There was a love in everything they did. For instance, when I got up next morning someone offered to make my bed for me. No-one had ever done that before. Another fellow offered to give me a massage when I was going through those shooting withdrawal pains. No-one told him he had to. Another one came to me and said, 'Listen, if you want to talk things over feel free, even if it's in the middle of the night; if you want to unload, just call me.' That really impressed me because no-one had ever given me that kind of treatment before.

I couldn't ignore the fact that in spite of the motley

mixture, there was a goodness that prevailed and somehow unified us all—even those of us who were cynical. Although there was a lot of talk about God and the Bible, it was never forced upon us—but to me what spoke louder than words were the leaders' lives. My curiosity was certainly awakened, but I was anxious just to go through withdrawal and be gone. Many times I made plans to leave the next day, but something always stopped me.

I missed my son Oscar so much. He was all that I had left now and he was ten hours away in Seville. He was another reason why I wanted to leave the centre—somehow I had to get him back. But how? In these difficult moments I would sense something inside of me saying, 'Alfredo, be patient and it will all work out.' At times, while listening to sermons, it seemed to me that God was actually talking to me and saying the words, 'Wait, and I will do it.' I desperately wanted to know this God that seemed so concerned about me and my situation. However, I was so timid that when an opportunity was given to go forward after the church service I would stay where I was.

The one thing from my past that weighed heavily on my mind was María del Mar's untimely death. My mother-in-law's parting words after the funeral were, 'You murdered my daughter.' The truth was that I introduced her to drugs some three years before. Her death was a lead weight on my conscience every waking moment. I wondered, 'How could God ever forgive me for what I've done?'

I would pray every night that God would return my son to me, but looking back, it was a demanding prayer—it was my 'right'. God showed me that I had no right to expect him to do anything, so my thinking changed. He spoke to me and said, 'You have to demonstrate that you are responsible, and can take care of him.' Eventually I prayed, 'I give my son to you. He's in your hands. I'm not going to worry about it.

I'm going to leave it with you.' As soon as I made that statement I had complete peace; there was no more struggle.

It was coming towards Christmas and one day Lindsay came to me and said, 'Why don't you ring up and see if your parents-in-law will let you have Oscar during the holidays —just for those two weeks.' I was scared to do it because I was sure they would say 'no', and so I didn't show much interest. Finally I plucked up the courage and rang.

This wasn't the first time I'd rung; at first my mother-in-law used to hang up and say 'wrong number'. Later they let me talk to Oscar, but they would put the words into his mouth. So I rang with fear and trembling. I had no indication that they would change their attitude.

When I got through I didn't even mention the subject. There was a different tone in my mother-in-law's voice and she said, 'Listen, we've been thinking that Oscar's place is really with his dad and we've decided not just to let him go to you for Christmas. We think it's time you had him back with you permanently.'

All that happened three years ago. I know I have arrived home finally, after a long, long journey. I feel that, as a person, I am now complete, and I desire with all my heart to serve God as a full-time worker. There is a certainty within me that he has something big prepared for me. I feel useful and fulfilled. I am one of the leaders here in Valencia. I daily experience the privilege of sharing what Jesus has done in me with other young heroin addicts. My greatest desire is to be one of his instruments here on earth.

10

'WOULD YOU LOOK AFTER MY BABY?'
The strange story of Blanca

For eighteen years Blanca had never lived with her daughter. For the past ten she hadn't even seen her, and now here she was on her doorstep—the girl whom she had entrusted to a stranger for all these years while she had indulged in a selfish and dissolute lifestyle. What would she think? How would she act? Probably much the same as Blanca herself did as a half-abandoned child.

Coldness is the one word that describes the family relationships of Blanca's youth. Every two years of her young life another brother or sister arrived until ten of them, plus parents, were packed into their tiny home in Pamplona. Noise and confusion reigned, one reason being that the authority figure of her father was mostly absent because his work was in Madrid, 300 kilometres to the south.

Her mother's work was never-ending, and in the absence of her dad (who came home only for the annual holiday), her older brother was actually the one who took his place. Not even uncles or aunts or grandparents seemed to take any interest in her. Blanca describes her reactions to all this:

Because we were such a big family, and money was so scarce, I was always looking around to see what others had —I would dream that one day I would be someone special and have plenty of everything.

I went to a Catholic school but was very rebellious, difficult to control, and always dreaming. I really was the black sheep of the family.

In my part of the country everybody drinks, and I can remember getting drunk at the age of five. As I grew up alcohol became my standby—I had to drink to face life. However, I resisted heroin even though other acquaintances took it. At sixteen, I found a job with our next door neighbour who owned two stores—a shoe store and a furniture store, side by side. I worked in both.

Blanca had a relationship with a travelling salesman who called regularly at the furniture shop. After a few months she found she was pregnant, and in her embarrassment decided to leave Pamplona and go to Valencia where she was admitted to a Catholic home for unmarried mothers. She continues:

As soon as the baby was one month old I packed my things and with 100 pesetas, a newspaper, and the baby, I set off for the city. I was eighteen by then.

I found a place to stay and then noticed the address of a child care centre. It was called BUBBY PARK. I went and inquired only to find it was very expensive. 'Would you look after my baby, while I try to find a job?' They agreed.

Again from the newspaper I found that the places that paid the best wages were clubs, so I managed to get a job in one. All I had to do was serve drinks, and after five days I had enough to pay off what I owed to the child care centre, expensive though it was.

I found another boarding house where the owner was willing to look after the child while I was at work. This lady had a close friend called Carmen who visited her frequently. Carmen developed a warm affection for my child, I think, partly because she had had three sons and badly wanted a girl.

I wasn't particularly impressed with the way my landlady cared for my daughter. It contrasted vividly with the affection Carmen lavished on her, so one day I asked her, 'Why don't you take her home and look after her? In fact— you can have her!'

She resisted strongly at first because she feared that this would create problems with her friend. (I was paying the landlady extra for caring for the child and this would mean a loss of income for her.) But eventually her feelings for the child triumphed and she took her.

About a month later I found a very smart flat in the city and moved there on my own. I continued to work in high class bars and clubs and managed to avoid serious involvement with men. Every week I would visit Carmen and pay her for keeping Ruth.

My flat became a hive of activity. Friends started to come around. I was an outgoing person that loved fun, laughter and parties, and as time went on I went to see Ruth less and less. By the time she was eight she had disappeared from my life completely.

It was when I was nineteen that I started to go downhill. I remember going to Ibiza and sniffing heroin for a week. The withdrawal after that, when I came home, was uncomfortable.

At the age of twenty-one, I began to sense a feeling of saturation, thinking I had tasted all there was to life. Perhaps this was a result of my promiscuous lifestyle. On the other hand, I felt a great vacuum within me because nothing around me held the remotest attraction for me any longer. By twenty-five I couldn't have a night's sleep without sleeping tablets.

For ten long years my dependence on pills and alcohol progressively increased. The physical and psychological deterioration was palpable and I hated being this way, but paradoxically I was unwilling to give up my lifestyle. I was

in an endless search for every new experience available—
the latest rock groups, becoming a punk, playing poker, the
sects, such as New Way and Guru Majarashi.

*Things became worse when she started going out with a man
who was hooked on heroin. She started taking it also,
thinking it would give her an escape from herself. After a
year and a half she came to the realisation that she was
totally hooked. This led to robbery and prostitution in order
to have enough money for the drug. She says she was very
timid so didn't rob often; it was easier to offer her body and
receive payment for doing so.*

*By thirty-five she was utterly desperate and booked into
a clinic which offered methadone therapy. For eighteen
months she continued to submit to this government control-
led and financed treatment, but it was destroying her health
and she had to be admitted to hospital seriously ill. She did
recover there, but on discharge fell back into her old ways.*

She says:

I went back to the doctor who had been administering the
methadone treatment—I told him I didn't want *any* drugs;
that I was willing to change my whole lifestyle or else I
would die.

Several days later another doctor from the Red Cross
gave me a card for Betel. He explained that it would be no
easy matter there because I would have to make a total break
with all the medicines and drugs that I had taken for many,
long years. He also spoke to me of the discipline this would
require: 'You really can't afford to bide your time. Take
what is offered to you and do it quickly.'

I recall the day I arrived at Betel. I was a terrible sight.
My hair was in matted bunches, all of different lengths,
because part of it had caught fire (I'd fallen asleep with my

head too close to a burning candle). My face was somewhat deformed from alcohol abuse and my features distorted due to psychological deterioration and a score of other excesses that accompanied my kind of lifestyle.

True to the doctor's word I found everything very different to begin with, but, conscious of my dreadful condition, it never entered my mind to quit. It took me a month before I managed to sleep four or five hours at a time. Some days I had no idea where I was.

All about me I heard people talking about God, which made me think that they were all a bit crazy. I didn't like the atmosphere either. I had become a person who rarely spoke. I lived in my own little world and wasn't interested in what was happening around about me. Just the same, something in my head told me that everything was going to work out OK.

Bian Tan, a Chinese missionary, was always there to help me. She was always trying to persuade me to come downstairs to read from the book of James or some other book of the Bible. I tried to keep out of her way and make excuses, but finally she got me down there and each day I'd go and read through the verses and chapters. Each time she'd ask me to tell her what I had learned from what we had read. I've always been a very philosophical person, I like things to be a bit complicated and Bian did her very best to make things so simple that in the end I'd say, 'Well, that's true, it is as simple as that.' I was shocked to find that life could be simple.

At first I rejected anything I heard about God, but little by little, without even realising it, I began to feel that the speaker in the devotional meetings was speaking directly to me! I began to sense that something was calling me, something was asking me to react. In a couple of these gatherings, I even felt my heart pounding. One day God's word very clearly showed me that there were two roads and

I would have to choose: the one a road I had already known, and the other unknown—the 'straight' road that God was offering me. When opportunity was given to respond to God's offer, I rose to my feet and surrendered my life to Christ.

The change begins

From then on my life began to change daily. I began to notice that my very character was slowly being moulded into the image of Jesus. My total outlook on life changed. Now I started to like *other* things. I even spoke differently. I have come out of my little world and I can take an interest in others now. I read Frank Peretti's book *Piercing the Darkness* and started to understand the power of prayer.

To be honest I was so happy with what was happening to me that I didn't even think about my daughter. I remember when we were together for a Sunday meal, Myk came up to me and said, 'What about your daughter?' It was like a blow to my heart. The following Sunday she asked the same question, and something in me began to say that unless I dealt with this part of my life that I'd tried to bury I would not be able to go further in my spiritual life. My daughter was eighteen by then.

One day I plucked up the courage and wrote a letter to Carmen. I didn't even know if she lived in the same house —it had been so long since I'd been there. In less than a week Carmen and my daughter, Ruth, suddenly appeared at the door! It was the strangest experience. We just looked at each other as if we had never met. I'm a cold person but my daughter is even colder. We gave each other the customary kiss, but I felt nothing. It was a most embarrassing situation. I know that it was curiosity that had brought her. She wanted to see what had happened to her mother; what she looked like; how she was living.

171

Since then I have tried to understand my daughter a little bit better. The coldness has continued, but there is something there. She wants to know me, but can't forgive me for what I did.

I have to take myself in hand to write or ring her; we have even gone together to a family wedding recently in Pamplona (my brother paid our fares). But I still feel that there's a cold wall between us, and my longing is to sit down and write a bit more, because the times I've visited her we've tended to talk about frivolous things, unimportant details. I feel that I want to unburden my heart to her in a letter and tell her what I'm thinking about the future, and how I really feel towards her.

Today I am the leader of the women's house here in Valencia and have a real concern for the girls. I also help out in the office. Like Paul I can say 'Forgetting what is behind and straining towards what is ahead I press on towards the goal ...'.

11

ANYTHING FOR MONEY
The Testimony of Julia Andreo

When a girl is one of seven children living in a poor neighbourhood of Madrid, and when her father is an alcoholic, it is just the easiest thing in the world for her to give in to peer pressure and start experimenting with drugs. By eighteen Julia Andreo knew it all. She was soon hooked and on the treadmill of criminal activity that would bring in the money to sustain her habit. Describing these days she says:

Whenever I saw a purse or a wallet lying around, especially my mother's or brother's, I just took money. Many a time I left mother without anything to buy food for the household. Any gold jewellery I saw I took and sold; any new clothes that any of the family had I took and sold as well. Once I'd exhausted all the supplies at home, I tried my neighbours —asking them for money, and never repaying them.

I started selling hashish and that helped me to make some money, but before long I was using all the hashish myself instead of selling it. I'd get together with a couple of others to rob people. We'd corner young people and say if they didn't give us money we'd do something to them. I can remember taking a gold chain from a woman while standing quite close to a police car. I had a courage and boldness to do anything for money.

Then I saw the only possible route was to make friends with men who sold hashish or heroin and I'd just do whatever they wanted, and I hoped that they would give me a fix in return.

I went to work at a club in Coslada, a suburb near San Blas. It had a bar and there were rooms with a bed. I wasn't obliged to go to bed with the men; in the beginning I would just persuade them to buy as many rounds of drinks as possible. The more drinks a client bought, the more the bar owner paid me. But there wasn't enough money in that so I said to myself, 'I may as well.' I was well paid for just a few minutes with these men.

I felt bad at first, but as soon as I had cash in my hands I felt great, so relieved that I didn't have to be scrounging for the next fix. I would go there at seven in the evening and not leave till three or four in the morning.

After a couple of months I met up with a young Austrian truck driver. He said he liked me and asked me to go to Austria for a trip—we would be back within three weeks, so off I went, without even telling my boss.

I didn't take any heroin. I just took tablets so I would not feel the pains of withdrawal, but as soon as I was back I went right on to heroin again.

The bar owner was upset at me leaving but he took pity on me and let me return. (I guess I helped to increase his profits.)

It was only a week after Julia had commenced her old job again when she heard about Betel from a family friend. She phoned the Madrid office, but when she heard there was a women's centre in Valencia she asked if she could go there so that she would be right away from her old haunts to which she would be tempted to return.

Julia continues:

Two of the Betel girls met me at the station in Valencia and took me to the hostel. I went there so heavily drugged that I fell over going up the stairs; they had to help me to the top.

A number of other girls were in various stages of rehabilitation; one of them burst into tears when she saw my helpless, stupefied condition. I slept right through that first night, but when I started to go through withdrawal sleep left me completely for several weeks.

I was put on light duties and one of my tasks was assembling little plastic toys. It was then that I met this Chinese girl, Bian Tan; she was working away there with the rest of us.

She always talked to me about the Lord, but that particular day she had a little note book and pencil with her and she was listening to us saying things like, 'I'm a mess.' Literally the Spanish means 'I'm made like dust' so she'd ask me, 'What's this about dust?' She was quite confused with all our slang, so I spent quite a bit of time explaining all these things to her.

I think what surprised me most about Bian was that when I asked her what she was doing there she said she was a missionary! I thought missionaries went to Africa and places like that. Also, missionaries to me were people 'way up there', very important. If we went out to sell these windscreen protectors she'd go with us, and if we had to do any menial task in the house, she'd do it too. She never complained. She was always with us, always ready to encourage us. She was the first one to pray with us if we had a problem, to sit down and identify with us.

The thing I'll never forget was watching her when a new girl came in; she was covered in terrible sores. Her head was shaved and it was covered in sores. She was a sight to see, and there was Bian just dressing all those wounds without any problem at all. She just got in there and loved and cared for us all.

Soon after that I discovered I was pregnant. For me, this was the end of the world; I was so distraught. But the others brought me flowers and said it was a blessing. I couldn't see it.

My first thoughts were that I would leave and have an abortion, but Trini and Marinella, the leaders, talked to me and said if I left I wouldn't have an abortion, I'd have a fix and end up being a drug addict again, but having a child as well. They just loved me so much that I thought, 'Well, I can't go. It's true what they're saying. This is going to be a blessing.'

I knew that God existed, but no-one had ever told me before that he could change my life and fill my heart with love. At the same time I began to realise that heroin was not my only problem, but rather there were lots of things that needed to change in me, and I couldn't do it alone.

One day when I was terribly depressed, I sincerely told God that I simply couldn't go on, and needed him to help me. I committed my life to Christ and from that very day my life began to change, thanks to Jesus. He has freed me from drug addiction and from all the other 'chains' holding me as well.

As soon as I had the baby I went to live with Lindsay and Myk McKenzie in their apartment, with their children, Rebecca and Priscilla, because the baby was so small and needed constant attention, but later I wanted to be a mum on my own so went back to the hostel.

I was there continually, caring for the baby, and so had a lot to do with the other girls and had to step into the shoes of Trini, the leader, because she was away practically all the time.

During this time I discovered that I was HIV positive and that my child would automatically be HIV positive too. But this knowledge caused me to trust and love Christ more because I could see his faithfulness in his dealings with me.

To cut a long story short, God healed my son—his antibodies to AIDS slowly disappeared and tests remain negative. I thank God for allowing me to be a mother and to look after my boy. But above all, I thank him for permitting me to know him and enjoy a new life with him.

Julia entered the centre in June, 1990 and when Trini, the leader, left to marry Tomás in April, 1992, she had matured to the point where she was asked to take charge of the women's side of the work.

In November, 1993, since this testimony was written, she was married to Juan Capella, leader of the work in Ceuta, North Africa. Their marriage and commitment to ongoing service for the Lord in Betel has made a deep impression on their parents and some of the wider family, although others are antagonistic to the One who has transformed their lives. A final word from Julia:

The first thing I said to Juan when he asked me to marry him was, 'You know that I'm AIDS positive, don't you?' He didn't care because he was certain that God wanted us together. He is negative to AIDS up until now. We feel, both of us, that since God has called us together we just have to trust him in this, whatever the outcome. The desire of my heart is to serve the Lord so that others can know him too.

12

BLIGHTED LIVES — BLESSED SERVANTS
The story of Juan Carrasco and Carmen

Here is the story of two strong characters. Whatever Juan Carrasco did, he did with all his heart. Before conversion he was totally given to heroin; he robbed a hundred apartments and many freight trains in order to have money to pay for his expensive activities. He ended up sleeping 'rough' with rats for company. The course of events leading to his conversion is dramatic—we can see the 'hound of heaven' at work. Now he is leader of one of Betel's most successful centres.

Carmen went the whole way in sin, mindlessly throwing off the good advice faithfully given her by family, friends and missionaries. But once in Christ growth was fast, leading to maturity and responsibility.

Juan grew up in a typical Madrid working class family. He is thirty-seven now, but when he was younger Spain was in dire economic straits and his father had to go to Switzerland for six months every year to find work. He was one of five brothers and his grandfather lived with them also. The eight of them were cramped into a small suburban flat.

He always did well at school. After his studies finished, as a teenager Juan worked for a while putting up television antennae on top of apartment buildings. Then the family moved to Torrejón near the American Air Force base.

Juan tells his own story:

By the time I was sixteen I was smoking marijuana and hashish, and from there I moved into the various drugs one can buy on the street. At that time the only thing that kept us reasonably stable was sport. I seemed to do well in soccer and actually advanced to playing with the third national division. But all that crumbled when I became more involved with the drug scene. I would disappear from home for three days at a time and was not prepared to accept the discipline needed for training.

From the age of sixteen I was going downhill—a descent into lower and lower forms of degradation. I managed to find a job in a bar, but of course that increased my consumption of alcohol.

I had to do national service in the army at eighteen and this led to more problems in dissolute living. I was put in charge of the canteen, which had a bar, so I used to rob up to 25 litres of gin and coke a night, then give it to my friends. They told me, 'Your supervisor won't be able to steal his supplies at the end of the month—you've already taken his share!'

When I left the military I found that my old friends had moved on to taking heroin. I did not want to become involved in that, so I started to use cocaine instead. I then moved on to dealing in all kinds of drugs, but after three months I was hooked on heroin myself.

Living near the American base it was easy to make money selling drugs to the airmen. People had the impression that Americans were selling drugs to the Spaniards, but the opposite was the case.

The Americans made far more money than Spanish people and it was easy to deceive them and cheat them. I was earning the equivalent of $300-400 a day, but as my addiction to heroin increased even that amount of money was not sufficient to buy what I needed. So I started into a life of crime. Once addiction happens one loses physical strength and there is no stamina for ordinary work.

I would go off with my partner and rob a flat, stealing, say, a kilo or two of jewels. We would sell this and immediately use the money for heroin. On the following day the process would have to be repeated. We would steal boxes of women's jewellery and sell it by the kilo. There was no set price, we would simply take it to crooked jewellers or to the black market. Sometimes we would rob five or six apartments a day.

I began to have problems with the police. Up to this point I did not have a criminal record because I had never been caught.

Once I was selling gold on the street when a special anti-burglary squad caught me. On interrogation my partner confessed that we had robbed one hundred flats in the Torrejón district, so we were both thrown into jail.

Prior to that I had been living with a woman and she had become pregnant. I remember one night in the jail I started to cry out to God, 'Take me out of here, God. I don't want my daughter to be born while I am in prison. I don't want her to have to come here to see me.' Well, after only six weeks I was released on bail through the help of a very good lawyer. This seemed so impossible, but God had really worked for me. However, once I was out I went right back to my old way of life.

The only thing that helped me was that I was now a father. That put a little bit of stability into my life; I calmed down and decided to look for a job.

I found one at the town hall. It was a good job. We had been living in a flat but it was damaged by a fire which started in the house next door. Through my contacts at the town hall I was given a beautiful new apartment that belonged to the government housing authority. I paid only $30 a month.

Things started to go better. I had my wife and my

daughter; I had a home, a car, a good job in the town hall and was the secretary of the business committee. I was the one who negotiated contracts with the private businesses on behalf of the city government. But even with all these assets I continued to inject myself with heroin.

I did not have to rob so much. In reality I simply robbed my family. My whole salary was spent on myself and I simply did not take care of them. They reached the point where living with me was impossible, so they abandoned me completely.

I went to what are called government 'day centres' where people try to break free of drugs with the help of doctors and psychologists.

I was so disturbed, so distraught, that once I even tried to throw myself out of a window in the psychologist's office. I moved to the window and was half way out when I stopped. They took me to a psychiatric hospital; it's easy to go in —you go in voluntarily, but it's pretty hard to get out once you're there.

When I left I didn't have anything, but everybody tried to help me, including the mayor of the city; he had been paying my salary into a bank account while I was in the hospital and he wanted me to come back to work. I went to the bank, withdrew the money, and spent it in two days on heroin. Eventually I lost my job at the town hall because of my irrational behaviour. Then I had to go back to robbing, even selling Kleenex at street corners. I had to sleep in an empty store full of rats. In the winter I would look for a little corner, a little niche, cover myself up with cardboard boxes and the clothes I had, and try to sleep. I lived like the homeless in New York, but nobody brought me food or gloves like they do there. This was Vicálvaro! I was a real 'homeless' vagabond.

Hound of heaven on his trail

Billy Glover, a WEC missionary, used to come by and give me a copy of 'VEN', a gospel paper. I used to take it, hoping that I could deceive him and perhaps persuade him to give me money.

One day I took out my wallet; it had a little card in it which said 'Mision Urbana'. To this day I don't know how it came to be there. I was in the habit of going to the Atocha railway station in the city, in order to mingle with the crowds and rob people. I bumped into a pharmacist from Torrejón, and of all things, he started to talk to me about my need of Christ. It was really strange.

About this time I somehow managed to accumulate a little bit of money and was able to find a room in a cheap boarding house. One night I couldn't sleep so I decided to go to the out-patients' department at the hospital to see if I could persuade the doctor to give me a prescription for a few tranquillisers. I was successful and soon had the prescription, but since it was the weekend, and all the shops were closed, I had to go to the central pharmacy for the district.

Wonder of wonders, the pharmacist on duty was the Christian who had testified to me at the Atocha station! My first thought was, 'This is great, he'll be easy to deceive. I'll tell him I have no money and he'll give me the drugs, free.' I gave him my story and he said, 'I'll give you the drugs, but I'm also going to give you a telephone number; I want you to call this man because he can help you.'

I rang and talked to Keith Bergmeier, a WEC missionary, who lived in Concepción. It seemed as if everyone wanted to talk to me about Jesus! Anyway, I went to see him at his home. He was very considerate and let me have a shower. After that, his wife gave me something to eat, and he went on to say, 'I will find you a place in our centre.' I replied, 'I have been shooting drugs for eleven years and

I've never tried one of these centres before.'

It was interesting that this was the first home I had been in where I had no desire to steal anything. I left them with the promise that I would turn up next day and go with him to this place.

So I met him, but I told him that I would have to go to say goodbye to my family. In actual fact they hadn't seen me for four years and didn't care what might happen to me. The truth is that I still had some money and wanted to have one last fix, so off I went to Vallecas where I bought heroin, and once that was in my veins I forgot about Keith and went back to my old ways.

Well, finally I reached the end of myself. I was absolutely penniless, and decided that I simply had to seek help. I went to the Metro station and asked the ticket lady to let me through. 'I don't have any money, but I must board the train because I have a serious problem; if you let me through I can solve it.'

It was ironic. After eleven years of dealing and robbing everywhere, even making two trips to Amsterdam to buy big quantities of drugs, I had finally reached a point in my life when I seriously wanted to be cured, and I didn't have the few pesetas to take me to the rehabilitation centre.

'Call the police; call the guards, if you like. I don't care. I'm going through.' So I finally managed to reach the Bergmeier's place.

They invited me in and I remember sitting down to eat with this family. They had a little blonde-headed girl, about five years old, and she's the one who helped me stop smoking. After the meal I took out my cigarettes, and little Carla said, 'Dad, look; the man smokes!' She said it in such a way that I felt ashamed. I put it out and I've never smoked another cigarette since.

That same day they took me to Betel. It was a Wednesday and a meeting was in progress. I had torn dungarees, long hair, and was filthy. My trousers were stained with blood from shooting up. I had a big bottle of tranquillisers and a syringe full of blood in my pocket. I didn't even know what I was carrying because I was so out of my mind. I had no spare clothes—just what I stood in. The person in charge was Carlos. He examined me, took all the stuff out of my pockets and gave me a body search. He asked, 'Why are you bringing this kind of stuff here?'

He then asked if I had any criminal charges against me. I said, 'Yes, I was arrested and tried for robbing one hundred apartments. The fellow who was with me was given six years, but they have never called me in to sentence me after being released on bail. I have never heard from them again. I don't know what happened.' It was then that I realised how marvellously God had answered my prayer to be released.

Then I remembered there was another judgment concerning the national railroad company when we had been robbing the trains. This is a federal offence. The equivalent of about $220,000 had been robbed from freight cars and I was among the group of people that was charged with it. That judgment disappeared also and I never heard any more about it. This happened eight years earlier and the other episode eleven years ago. It seemed as if my convictions had just been forgotten, overlooked or pardoned.

The day I entered Betel something happened—just like when that little girl spoke to me about the cigarette. I never looked back. I remember the first time I was allowed to go home. I was accompanied by my shadow. They offered us wine but I just drank water. Everything had changed. I recall starting to get drunk when I was nine years old. I stayed on that road until I was thirty.

Nothing and no-one can change you if God doesn't change you. As soon as I entered Betel and started listening to God, my life started to move in a new direction. Mind you, I had a very bad time during the withdrawal period. I really suffered physically then, and continued to have a bad time for months afterwards as my body tried to adjust to normal living.

But as far as being tempted to go back to drugs or smoking or drinking, I never had any more problems. I'm persuaded that when I finally gave myself to Jesus he gave me a new life. I'm persuaded that he burned all those legal judgments against me so that I could really enjoy the new relationship I have with him.

Carmen, Juan's present wife, came from Cuenca where her parents were fruit sellers. She went to school until she was fourteen and then started work, selling fruit with her father in the markets and living a normal teenager's life. When she was seventeen things became more difficult. She started to go to the discos and in just one year everything changed. She took up smoking, and used hashish, marijuana, amphetamines and even LSD on holidays or festivals. She wasn't a regular drug addict, but by her eighteenth year she was hooked on amphetamines and started to have hallucinations. She felt she was losing her mind and finally fled from home.

She continues in her own words:

I returned home every once in a while but didn't stay any length of time. Then I met a fellow and we went off together to Madrid where I became pregnant. The relationship did not work out so I returned to my family. After the child was born I stayed for about three months and then took off again, leaving the baby for my parents to look after.

I lived with one of my girl friends called Lourdes who had been a drug addict for about three years. She gradually drew me into her world. It was during another trip to Madrid that I started to inject heroin, and that was the start of a five

185

year nightmare. I had to steal to get money to maintain my habit and did a lot of shoplifting, selling the stuff I had stolen. I also started dealing in hard drugs. This went on until I was twenty-five.

It was Juan Torres, a WEC missionary in Cuenca, who told me about Betel. He used to plague me with the idea of going there. He said my life could be totally changed. We always seemed to be bumping into each other, but I never paid any attention to what he said. I would just walk off and leave him.

One day I was in my parents' home and was having a bad time. I couldn't eat and I couldn't sleep, in fact I was passing through withdrawal. I felt so bad I just did not know what to do. I turned to my parents and said, 'Please call that man who has been talking to me about Betel. I need help.' Juan called Betel in Madrid and made arrangements for me to be admitted the next day.

When I arrived there, a meeting was going on and the people seemed really strange. I was put under the care of a lady called Marimar. She seemed to be an extremist, always raising her hands and praising the Lord. I wondered what I was in for!

After the meeting we went off in a van, crushed in like sardines. I wondered what lay ahead of us. They took me to this house which seemed to be full of beds. They searched me and went through my clothes. It was all so strange, and for the first twenty days I kept telling myself, 'I'll stay for just one more day, then move out.' For the first fifteen of these days I simply could not sleep, but after that time I began to feel better and went out with the girls on work schedules. I started to sleep and the days seemed to become shorter and not so hard. So I decided I would stay for two or three months. The simple truth is that if I had left, I had nowhere to go and nothing to do.

People were talking about God and I was willing to listen, but it did not make any sense. After two months I remember being in a meeting in the women's house. We were sitting round a big table in the dining room holding hands and praying. Suddenly I felt the Holy Spirit flowing into my body. From then on, things really changed. I still had struggles, but basically my life really altered and I became attentive to the truth of God's word. I started to take things seriously and to head in the right direction.

After eight months I started to do serious and rewarding Bible study, and when the leaders saw this they invited me to join the Adullam Bible School several afternoons a week.

There were not many girls in the centre and even less leaders, so I was given responsibility quite early. This helped to bring more maturity.

When I had to look after others I was also ministering to myself, because what I told them to do I had to be sure I did myself. This experience pushed me on to the Lord and I began to learn how to pray. Actually I was a pretty rough type and often had to be corrected myself by a senior leader.

My principal fault at that time was wanting to be a friend to the girls rather than being their pastor. I would not exert discipline because I was so undisciplined myself. With my background of laziness and rebellion I did not create an orderly atmosphere for these girls. Other staff workers had to straighten me out so that I could help them.

After I had been in Betel for a year a strange rumour circulated in Cuenca. Raúl Casto saw a newspaper article saying that I had died of AIDS. He called the editor and said, 'This can't be true; she's been in our centre for one year and one month,' so the newspaper decided to investigate the case. They interviewed my parents and then two cameramen, a reporter and my father made the two-hour trip to Madrid to interview me. I was able to give my testimony, and it was published in the only daily newspaper in the province of Cuenca. It made a tremendous impact.

After a while God began to speak to me about Juan Carrasco and show me that he could be the man for me, but I didn't like the way he behaved. He was always shouting, always very gruff and tough. He was in charge of food distribution and was really stingy, never giving any more than the minimum to the girls. Someone broke into the food store and stole some very expensive cured hams we had been given. My reaction was: 'It serves him right; he's so mean.'

I decided to talk to two of the leaders, Tito and Isabel, about my feelings and they gave me their counsel: 'Just keep praying about it and asking the Lord to show you what he wants.' I did this, and the more I prayed the more sure I became that it was right.

Juan continues:

I remember I had to make a trip to Cuenca. Tomás, Trini, Jambri and Carmen were going too. Up till this time I had been greatly troubled about my relationship to my former wife; I had tried to find a way of reconciliation but had met with total rejection on her part. She was in the process of divorcing me. It was really destroying my peace. During the journey I began to notice Carmen and it occurred to me that she might be my future partner.

A whole year passed and I did not pursue the matter further, but after that I asked and was given permission to date Carmen.

Elliott Tepper now takes up the story and gives a few explanations:

188

We allowed them to date because they were both behaving well and acting responsibly, but after three months we realised he was still legally married even though separated from his wife for more than two years. In Spain a two year separation must precede divorce. Juan's wife had started divorce proceedings but the matter was still before the courts. Technically he was still married, so we had to step in and tell him he could not go out with Carmen. He was angry at us for doing this.

It was a classic case of trying to sort out the confusion, the destruction, the fruit of sin in people's lives. It just can't be cancelled out right away.

Here were two people, new creatures in Christ Jesus, wanting to make a new start. Carmen couldn't find the man who fathered her child. Juan couldn't achieve reconciliation with his former wife who had his child. They felt that God was wanting them to form a new family, but we had to sort everything out.

We had to delay, honour the civil law, and, of course, have biblical grounds for divorce and remarriage. This led us to form a policy and set rules for dating and marriage. We came to see that all their sins, broken promises, broken covenants, selfishness, immorality and unfaithfulness—even divorce—before conversion were under the blood and forgiven, but once they crossed into new life in Jesus, we held them to the highest biblical standards enunciated by the Lord in the tenth chapter of Mark. If members of the community were still married—even though separated from their former partner—they could not date; furthermore we said they couldn't even begin a relationship until they were eighteen months old in the Lord. In the early days we didn't have those rules and were only feeling our way. We were very much like the church at Corinth, trying to build a church out of wrecked lives.

189

Juan's divorce finally came through and they were married one year later. They had a long wait.

Juan and Carmen are now in charge of our work in Barcelona. They are outstanding leaders and the various departments that make up the total operation there are most fruitful and productive. God has taken over Juan's natural capabilities and transformed them for both commercial and spiritual effectiveness.

13

THE LONG SEARCH
The story of Manolo and Mari Carmen

The story of Manolo is a tremendous example of the total transformation that the gospel can bring. He had a home life saturated in hatred and violence: a heartless mother who caused the death of his father; he moved into robbery with violence and the turmoil of gang life ending up with a four-year prison sentence. All the time something inside was crying for acceptance, love and peace. The long search ended when he finally met the Lord in the Betel community.

Mari's background is just as horrific. Clubs and knives used in the home: a dissolute and incestuous father. Then, after marriage to Manolo, she becomes what he describes as 'the best drug dealer in San Blas'. With the appearance of pure innocence she pushes drugs as she pushes the baby carriage, heroin hidden in the diapers!

Manolo gives his story first:

I was the seventh child in a family of eight. My father was an alcoholic. He and my mother were continually fighting —insulting and abusing each other. At one stage I had thoughts of suicide; I felt there was no meaning to life, only suffering and fighting. I found an escape from this hatred and emotional turmoil by joining gangs. I became a gang leader and formed my own group. For this kind of activity I was thrown out of school at thirteen.

I tried to find work but I was so young I did not know how to behave; I was too immature and lost my first few jobs. Instead, I just lived in the gang world. The only release I had from frustration was to have a fight; I was constantly beating up people in my neighbourhood.

I started to use and sell hashish when I was eighteen; then I had to do military service. When I came out, I found that the gang had broken up and work was difficult to obtain, so I ended up selling heroin.

About that time I met Mari Carmen. We started going out together but she did not know then that I was an addict. I began to coax her to have a 'snort'—a sniff, but not to inject; she would comply every once in a while. For the first three years I did not inject either. You use more when you sniff it, so I was using more than three grams a day. At that time one gram was worth 12,000 pesetas ($100).

Trafficking made me rich, but when I began to inject, everything went to ruin. I had to sell off everything I had— gold, cars, house, the lot. For the first three years I had made money, but for the next five I could only make ends meet. After that I had to rob to maintain my habit; my usual practice was to break into shops at night.

I was caught and sent to prison with a four year sentence. The charges were 'assault, intimidation and robbery'. Then I was released because my brother paid a bond for me, but that arrangement fell through because he was arrested at London airport for smuggling heroin and sent to prison in Britain for five years.

My mother took advantage of this. Because of my brother being in jail the bond was cancelled and she claimed the money back, with the result that I had to return to prison. Just imagine the state of relationships in my family when my mother would do a thing like that!

My father was still an alcoholic and his health was poor. In his weakness my mother would beat him up continually. One day he came home drunk and insulted her. She became very angry, grabbed him by the shirt and pushed him from the first floor, all the way down to the bottom. I tried to grab him and save him, but I couldn't hold him so he broke a number of bones, including his hip; they had to take him to hospital and operate. Since he was inebriated they couldn't put him under anaesthesia, so they had to operate with him conscious and when he began to detoxify, he lost control of his mind.

Within six months of the accident he died never having recovered from that fall down the stairs. I remember as they were burying him, my mother was throwing invective at him over his grave, saying he was never going to hurt or insult her again. Even in his death she was still fighting!

While my bond was still effective in 1984, before going back to jail, I met Elliott Tepper for the first time. He, Lindsay and Billy Glover were evangelising in San Blas. They used to go out with a sketch board, draw pictures and preach about Jesus. I remember Elliott talking to me about the Lord and I told him to get lost, or I would stab him. (I always carried a knife in my boot.) He didn't pay much attention because he came back next day and talked to me again.

Elliott was very insistent and came back once more, so I began to ask him some questions. 'What kind of God can this be who permits all this hunger and suffering and misery?' He kept on talking about the love of God and he invited me to his house for a meeting. I didn't want to go but he kept on insisting, so I went out of curiosity. Actually it was really more than curiosity because I thought if I went maybe I could get some money from him by thieving—and more than once I did.

Once we were in Elliott's house watching a movie called *Jesus of Nazareth*. In the middle of it Jesus was rebuking the Sadducees and I started to laugh. Elliott asked me why I was laughing and I said, 'Well, Jesus is right; they are a bunch of hypocrites and Jesus is giving them what they deserve.'

There was no Betel centre in Madrid at that time so he persuaded me to go to a centre in Vitoria. Elliott took me there seven or eight times (a 350 kilometres trip each way) but I would leave just as I had arrived—uncured.

In between these periods at Vitoria, Elliott would visit Mari Carmen and me in our home. I remember one of these in a special way. He brought Miguel Diez, the director of REMAR, with him. Most of our windows were broken and we had cardboard in the frames. My arm was bandaged; in fact it was swollen up like a balloon and full of blood clots. I could have died any time.

In the half light Miguel prophesied over me saying, 'My son, the devil has desired to sift you as wheat, but I have prayed for you. And when you are tried you shall come forth as gold.' Back then it sounded more like a fantasy than a prophecy.

During all this time Mari Carmen was also on drugs, strung out, apathetic and listless. She didn't bother about anything, in fact we had to ask my sister to take over the care of the children. Sarah was three, Israel one and Maria just four months old.

At one point in 1984 I had no money for a fix and was going through withdrawal. I was so desperate that I stole an electric toaster from my mother when she was not at home. She went off to the police and denounced me, with the result that they sent me a written charge. I said to my mother, 'I don't understand what this means,' so she said she would go to the police station with me to straighten it out. She did not tell me she was the one who had originated it!

At the police station the secretary told me I would be detained. I said, 'What for?' He answered, 'Because your mother denounced you for stealing the toaster.' The police were right behind me and grabbed me. My mother said, 'I

194

don't know what this is all about.' She lied; she had started the whole process. She wanted me out of her hair for a few months.

Through the witness and the love shown to me by the Betel people I realised they had something I needed, so eventually in 1986, when I came out of jail, I went to see them. Actually I arrived without making any previous arrangement. I stood there with my bag of clothes and they would not admit me because I had deceived them so often. So I just bedded down at the church entrance overnight and in the morning, seeing my determination, Lindsay relented and took me in, filthy and smelly as I was.

Even though Manolo was under Betel's influence over the succeeding months, he would not take the word of God seriously. He always had a hankering for the old life— discos, pubs, drink and drugs. After about a year he was sentenced to two years in prison for a crime he had committed before going to Betel. He had actually stolen electronic goods valued at 1,800,000 pesetas. While there he behaved so well that he was allowed out on occasional weekends, and at these times he would go straight to Betel and avoided drugs.

Manolo describes what happened during the closing months of his sentence:

One day in the twentieth month, I was on my bunk in prison. I was looking at a picture of my wife and children on the wall and was just thinking and meditating. I went outside to the balcony by myself and I heard this voice that said to me, 'Manolo, you belong to me; your life belongs to me.' Then he said, 'Look around you; look at those convicts around you.' I looked and saw one man who was trying to get some drugs from another; a second was robbing the possessions

195

of his room-mate; three others had taken a fourth into the bathroom to beat him up. I was surrounded by corruption. The voice said to me, 'What you are seeing right now is the life that you have led. Decide now if you are going to continue doing all these evil things, or to follow me.'

In that moment my heart was broken and I started to cry. One of the prisoners looked at me and said, 'What's the matter with you? What's happened to you, Manolo?' I told him that nothing had happened, but inside I made my decision to serve God, I didn't want that life of wickedness and evil any more; I chose God.

I asked to have some leave, and they gave me an eight day pass. I went to Madrid, and my heart was set on entering Betel because if I didn't I knew what was waiting for me in the street. When I reached my neighbourhood and I saw my wife I knew that I wanted to go straight, so I talked to Raúl Casto about entering Betel. He told me it was going to be really hard because I wouldn't be able to smoke or drink. But I said, 'No, I really want to do it,' and for those eight days I lived there.

I then had to go back to jail, but in another six weeks I asked for another eight days' leave and they let me out again. This time, rather than going straight to Betel, I fell into temptation. I went back to drugs, was caught by the police and put in the local jail for four days—all because I didn't keep my promise to God. I was in real danger. God told me that this was just the beginning of what would happen if I didn't obey.

I went back to prison, finished my 26 months, and was then released. I arrived in Madrid about nine o'clock at night. My wife was already in the centre, so I went to see my children and then called Betel and told them I wanted to come in right away. The next morning I arrived and I've been in the work ever since.

Manolo's wife, Mari Carmen gives her side of the story.

I was born into a very humble family in San Blas. My father was an alcoholic, but my mother was a very hard working woman. I can't say very much about my father because my last memory of him was when I was seven. My family fought with clubs and knives. Sometimes Dad would come home, take the food my mother had prepared, and throw it on the floor. There were five daughters plus myself and he was such a pervert that he started to violate his daughters sexually. Things were so bad my mother had to go to the courts to get him out of her life.

I went to school but I didn't study or pay any attention. Then at twelve I started to skip school, go to the parks and drink liquor. At thirteen my mother said if I wasn't going to study I had to work, so I left school and found a job in a printing house. I had a good mother and she tried to give me everything I needed.

After two years this printing establishment went out of business and I found another job working in a private home, cleaning. I started going to discos and became rebellious. Mother would give me a time to be home but I wouldn't keep to it. Sometimes I would stay away all night. I started taking LSD trips and lived a very disorderly life, going out with young men.

At eighteen I left home and went off to live with Manolo who is today my husband. I also started to take heroin then. We had a home in San Blas and we were trafficking in drugs with a sufficient margin to pay for our own consumption.

Manolo makes this comment about his wife:

Mari was one of the best drug dealers in San Blas. She sold more than anyone else. Although she looked like a sweet

197

little girl she was very astute and very tough. One time I was sick; I couldn't go out to rob and sell heroin, so she and two girl friends went out and robbed a store to make up for what I couldn't get that day.

When Mari Carmen was dealing in drugs she always looked so innocent. We used to hide the heroin in the children's diapers or the baby carriage and go through the streets. The police never searched her.

While Manolo was at Betel for the first time he was really worried about Mari for she was still on the streets, indifferent to the gospel. One day he said to Lindsay McKenzie, 'I am really burdened about my wife.' Lindsay replied, 'Well, let's go and look for her.' So Manolo, Lindsay and Raúl went round looking for her. They found her sitting in the doorway of a building looking half dead, and Manolo said, 'If you don't come into Betel, you can forget about me and the children.' That really shook her and changed her attitude.

They offered to take her with them, so she ended up in Myk Hall's apartment and spent eight days with her. Then they sent her up to RETO because they did not have a proper place for girls at that time.

Mari continues:

I had voluntarily given up the children to Manolo's sister and she began the paperwork to legalise custody of them. I spent a whole year at RETO but never really took a serious interest in the gospel. I was straightened out physically but I wasn't saved spiritually.

I returned to Madrid and within two months was hooked again. During this time Manolo was in prison for two years and I was all alone. I didn't have the children; I didn't have any place to live; I didn't have any money. I had to look for my survival out on the streets. I had to sleep in cars, or in the fields. I was totally abandoned.

During an eight day leave from prison Manolo talked me into going to the centre to be straightened out, so I went in again, and started to hear and understand the gospel. Slowly and gradually I came to a saving knowledge of the Lord Jesus Christ.

In 1990, with our lives straightened out, we started on the paperwork needed in order to have the children returned to us, but Manolo's sister would not agree. She had developed an affection for them and did not really trust us or feel that our cure was real and long-lasting.

The government insisted that Manolo should have a regular job, a regular income, and proof that we could maintain the children. We responded by saying that we wanted to continue to serve in Betel, helping other people who were in the same condition we had been in.

Elliott describes what happened:

I wrote a number of letters and explained that they were receiving the equivalent of $1,100 a month from the community, taking into account the value of their apartment, their fuel and food, the use of a car, and other personal allowances. I also gave them a glowing but honest character recommendation.

The government sent back a letter saying that according to its reports they were both still drug addicts, both still on the street, and still deceivers. But this judgment was based on a social worker's report dated 1986, so I had to write another letter and go personally with Manolo to the authorities. I said, 'You're making a judgement in 1991 based on a 1986 study of their lives.' They recognised that it was an error, reviewed the case, and returned the children to them.

199

Manolo and Mari Carmen have their lives and family together; they love the Lord with all their heart and are serving him. Manolo is a professional metal worker and used to be in charge of our workshop. He worked on doors, windows, gates, and all metal products. While in Madrid he was also the head of our drama team and he's one of our best street evangelists, preaching right from his heart to the people. Even though he may not be a student, he has a gift of communicating the gospel and is a very, very powerful speaker.

Mari Carmen became one of our principal secretaries. She handled the cash book, registering all the money in and out; she is trustworthy in every sense of the word and is one of the female leaders.

When the work in Barcelona began to grow we transferred them and their family there to work alongside Juan and Carmen Carrasco. Manolo is in charge of the metal shop and of evangelism. Marie Carmen used to work in the office but now she's more and more involved with the three children.

The first time that Manolo became aware that he had the AIDS virus was in 1988. The government gave him a health test in jail and he wasn't surprised when he heard the results.

Mari Carmen found out about her condition in 1987. She had a test when she was still on the streets and the result didn't surprise her. She didn't really know what it was, so it didn't have any impact on her life at that time.

In one sense this hasn't really changed Manolo's life because he knows that all men are going to die whether of AIDS or other things, but since he is a Christian he has hope. He recognises that the reason they're suffering is because of their wicked ways in the past.

Mari Carmen had a very bad bout of tuberculosis three years ago; she lost weight, her defence system was weakened and she was so anaemic that her life was in danger. She had all kinds of bumps and tumour-like things growing on her hands and feet. Miraculously they have all disappeared and all other secondary diseases are in total remission. More recently, seven months ago, she had candida (a fungus) in her throat, which is very serious and can cause blindness. That, too, has totally disappeared. To look at her today one would never know that she is HIV positive and has had life-and-death struggles with AIDS.

14

DEATH HAS NOT ROBBED US OF PEACE
The story of José Gonzalez and Mari Carmen

Here is the tragic story of a middle-aged couple who lost both a grown-up son and daughter to drugs, yet their new found faith in Christ remains intact. But we begin the saga when their own marriage is on the rocks. Mari describes the situation:

In 1976 my husband, José, and I, with our three children, lived in San Fernando outside of Madrid. José was working for a transport company loading and unloading trucks. The atmosphere in the home was very bad. We were at the point of separating. José was drinking. About half of his salary went on that. I was working at home. During the day he would drink; then he would come home from work, leave his things, and go off to the bar. Later he would come home drunk and very aggressive. He often hit me, and so I wanted to leave him.

At that time in Spain there was no divorce and I had the responsibility of my children and my home. If I left, I would have to leave them behind. I didn't know what to do. I loved my children and could not leave them, so I put up with it for years. But there came the day when I couldn't stand it any more. I told the two oldest children they would have to decide whom they were going to go with. They cried quite a bit over that.

One of my neighbours sent for a priest and when he came I told him about our problems. He said, 'Well, there's no divorce; you're together for better or worse.'

At this point I took out a magazine that I had read about Spanish artists. Some of them had been divorced and remarried and I showed the priest this. I said, 'How come these folks are divorced and remarried?' His response to me was, 'Well, you don't have a million pesetas ($10,000) to pay the Pope for an annulment.' I had always believed in God and I believed that priests were his representatives, but at that moment I rebelled. I said to him: 'Listen, if this is your God, then I don't want you or him, or your church. If I have to pay you a million pesetas, that's a year's work; and with that much money, I could solve these problems myself. I could go off and buy my own apartment and take my kids with me.'

José was there with me and the priest asked, 'Is there any affection between you two?' I told him how much I hated my husband and that whenever he touched me it was as if the worst bug I could think of had crawled across my chest. I just couldn't stand it. I remember one day he had an accident on his motorcycle. My reaction made me realise just how much I hated him. When I heard he was involved in a crash I instantly had a sense of relief and eagerly asked, 'Did he die?'

The priest left and I remember going to bed and crying. I just wished I had some feeling for José, but I knew I didn't, so I decided to leave.

Billy Graham film speaks to her heart

At home I used to earn money by waxing ladies' legs. A girl came by one day and I was so desperate that I spilled out my story. She was an evangelical who was attending a church at Pueblo Nuevo. She invited me to see a film that was being shown in a home in Coslada, a nearby suburb. I was desperate to get out of the house so I took the two children and went to see it.

It was the Billy Graham film *Time to Run*. In essence this film was the story of my life. I'd always thought that money would solve my problems, the central character in the film was a millionaire scientist. His family was coming apart, yet he had all the money he needed. His wife felt abandoned because he was working so much. At the end of the film the family came to know Christ through the witness of a friend. But what I remember most was that money wasn't the answer. Even rich families come apart.

At that point I didn't understand that the answer was Christ, but I suddenly realised money wasn't the issue. As the film ended I began to cry and someone touched me from behind and said, 'I see you have a problem. Do you believe that Jesus can help you?' I responded, 'If he doesn't then there's no hope for me.' We were in a big dining room with more than twenty people and I didn't know anybody. I had arrived after the film had started and I was crying, heaving and sobbing in front of all these people.

The pastor came over and a few people laid hands on me. I didn't understand this sort of thing. I'd never heard the gospel. But when they prayed for me, I felt a wonderful sense of release in my heart. I left there a different person. The Lord had met me and had done something in me that night. I've never gone back from that point.

When I arrived home I had an irresistible urge to put my arms around my husband and hug him. I suddenly saw things in reverse. We'd been blaming each other and all of a sudden I saw the good in him and the bad in me.

I couldn't sleep, so later that night I picked up the Bible from the shelf. Previously, when I used to read it I would fall asleep immediately. But I opened it up to the Psalm that says, 'As the deer pants for the streams of water so my soul longs after you,' and I knew that was exactly how I felt. I turned to another page and it said, 'If you believe with your heart and confess with your mouth that Jesus Christ is Lord, you will be saved.' I'd never seen that before.

Some time later I went to another film and afterwards the pastor said, 'Is your husband home? May I take you home and meet him?' We went home together, and he met José. The pastor then invited us to church, so we went together the following Sunday. I told José that I liked it and wanted to keep going every Sunday. So we did, attending both the morning and evening services. But although José was willing to go he was basically just doing it for my sake.

José takes up the story:

What impressed me most was this: as soon as I entered the church I sensed the difference in the atmosphere. There was such joy and peace; it was such an extreme contrast with what I was used to in the world. We went along like this for three or four months and then Mari decided she should be baptised.

Mari continues:

The fellowship used to have films regularly and I remember seeing one the night before my baptism. Some tribal people had killed several missionaries and the film later showed interviews with the men's widows. It was very moving.

As soon as it was over the pastor asked me, 'Now, Mari, are you ready for your baptism tomorrow?' I thought getting baptised meant that maybe I would have to be a missionary and risk my life, going to another country. I said, 'Lord, I don't know if I can face that.' So I told the pastor I didn't want to be baptised. When he asked me why, I said, 'Well, if I have to go and be a missionary like those people, I could not do it.' He laughed and told me that the Lord would never put me in a situation that was beyond my capabilities.

José picks up the story at this point:

At the baptismal ceremony I did not know what to expect, so when they immersed her in the water I jumped up out of my seat, thinking they were going to drown her. I had no idea what was happening.

All this time I did not realise I had a major problem that needed to be dealt with. I just liked going to church. I liked the people; I saw that their lives were better than those in the world. The pastor regularly asked the congregation if there were any present who wanted to receive Christ. At last one day, I said I needed him, so they prayed for me and my life began to change.

Mari now tells us about the family:

By this time my son José was fourteen and a half, María Luisa was twelve and Mari Carmen was five. They all came to church with us. We were finally a happy family. I even started to help at a drug centre which was being developed by Daniel del Vecchio in Madrid.

Things went really well for José and me after our conversions, until my son reached eighteen. At that time he had an accident on his motor cycle. He was crippled at the knee and limped badly. From then on, he started to develop a complex and had a bitter, negative attitude towards life. From helping out at the drug centre I knew the signs of addiction and was horrified to see these in my son. He had started to smoke marijuana and was drinking.

María Luisa left school at fourteen and we sent her for a year to England, where she lived with a missionary couple

206

as a member of their family. When she came back she testified to being born again, but I was not convinced. She found a good job here as a bilingual office worker because she spoke English so well.

Then at fifteen she started hanging around with her brother's friends. It wasn't long before she was exhibiting the same symptoms as José and I knew she had started to take drugs. They would both say to me, 'Well, mother, we've been to church this morning; must we go back in the afternoon? Can't we go out with our friends?'

At seventeen, earning a good salary, she went deeper into drugs, having strange hallucinations at night. For instance, she said she felt bugs crawling all over her. It was very difficult to know what to do.

When José was about twenty-three and still single he had a son Reuben. He began to use heroin and I saw the shot marks in his arm. He used to bring his drugged friends to me for help, and I would say, 'I'm helping them; what about you?' He would say, 'Oh, I don't need help, Mum. I'm OK. I'm not like these guys.'

So I helped a lot of his friends at that time, taking them to the REMAR centre here in Madrid. Our church people didn't know what I was going through because they didn't have the same problem. They saw I was sad but they didn't understand.

Then I met Elliott at the Pueblo Nuevo church when he came to speak. I saw that he understood drug addicts and had a heart to talk to the young people, so I asked him to come and talk to my son. There was something noble about him; he came and talked to him a number of times. He called the RETO centre in Santander, arranged for him to be admitted, and we took him up. He really met the Lord there.

José was in Santander three months. He was tested for AIDS and the results came back positive, so he came back to Madrid. He was really a prodigal son returning home. With his new values, he approached his girlfriend (the one who had the son) and asked her to marry him. She said 'no' and he came back crying because he was very sensitive. He said, 'It's not worth fighting.' I tried to encourage him. He wanted to re-unite his family, but when she refused he fell back into drugs. At one point he said he would go into Betel, which was newly opened, but he never did, and from that point onwards his health really started to go downhill. After living on the streets for nearly a year he died.

I remember the peace the Lord gave us then. God really surrounded us. Whereas people of the world scream and throw themselves about in mourning, we just had a peace together; we knew our son had sinned and died because of that, but we accepted it. It was God who kept us going.

Maria Luisa goes to Betel
For six months after José's death María Luisa continued to take heroin. She was living with a man called Luis. I pled with them to consider going for help. Meanwhile, they were married, and shortly afterwards space for them became available at Betel. Luis went to the men's house and María Luisa went to the girls', looking ghastly—she was so ill and emaciated with AIDS.

She was there for only twenty-one days and then had to go to hospital. She stayed for a whole month. At the end of that time she was so weak she could not go back to the centre, so she came to stay with us at home. Luis, meanwhile, continued at Betel.

She was with us three and a half months. We changed churches at that time and began attending meetings at Betel. After that time Luis decided to leave the centre and come to care for his wife, so they both went to their own home. She attended the Betel church and was baptised there. But she never regained her health, and after three and a half years she had to return to hospital, where she died. The pastor who was with her at the end said she passed away with a wonderful peace in her heart. Luis had been very faithful all that time and had worked diligently as a painter to support them both.

Our children were not bitter that they were ill and dying so young. They both testified at different times, 'We brought this situation on ourselves by our rebellious lifestyle. We are going to be with Jesus, which is far better, so don't be sorry for us.'

The one who was really hurt most by all this was our daughter, Mari Carmen, who was fourteen when her brother died. She began to ask me regularly, 'Mum, why do we, the people of God, have to suffer worse things than other people around us?' She went through a time of rebellion, questioning everything and wanting nothing to do with the church.

The third fiery trial

But she came to real faith in the Lord and has never gone into drugs. A year after María Luisa died, Mari Carmen married Miguel Jambrina, a worker with Betel, but soon after that came my third fiery test. They were both in a terrible car accident and she nearly died. The doctors had to operate twice, and they very much doubted if she would survive.

After they told me this, and with the memory of José and María Luisa, I went through a few seconds of doubt, but then all I had to do was look back at my own conversion and remember what had happened to me. I said, 'Yes, Lord. You are real. Forgive me for doubting.'

I look back now to the time when I was facing baptism and almost refused because I would not have been able to go through what these missionaries in the film had to endure. Well, here I am still strong in faith, and I reckon I can say I have been through as deep waters as they. God's grace is totally sufficient.

I feel that I couldn't live without the church. We could take what we have, sell our house and move to a place we own on the coast. We could just live there and take it easy, but I couldn't do it. I would be lost without the church and the fellowship.

15

PILAR'S AGONY
The story of Mrs Pilar Cano Minano of San Blas

Of all the testimonies heard by the writers, this was one that touched us most deeply and in fact left us in tears. We sat enthralled as Pilar related the tragic events of her life. At one stage she was visiting four of her children, all in different prisons at the same time. One son was shot and killed by the police. Another daughter, who was rehabilitated and found the Lord, died of AIDS.

Yet, in the midst of this nightmare she came to faith in Christ through attending Betel church. Today she stands firm, praising the Lord for his grace and rejoicing that at least some of the family have come to salvation.

We start at the point when her husband deserts her and the seven children.

I thought my marriage was going reasonably well until, one day, my husband left me. For years I had earned a good salary working for a very high class tailor. I met many famous people, such as the Kennedys, Gary Cooper and the Minister of Justice. It was through the help of the last-named that I was able to place the five oldest children in boarding schools. I kept the two youngest at home till they were of school age. They went to a nursery while I continued to work. My husband agreed to send support for us, but he never did. I went to live with my parents in another part of Madrid but saw the children every weekend.

When I returned to live in my own flat after ten years, my eldest daughter was going out with a young Dutchman. She married him and went to live in Amsterdam. The rest of us lived in our apartment in San Blas.

José started to take drugs when he was sixteen and a year later he was shooting up with heroin. One day I came in and found him counting money. I said, 'Where did you get all this?' He said, 'Oh, we found it.' The truth was that they had robbed a bank. Pretty soon the police arrived and he went to prison for a year.

Miguel Angel became involved in drugs at fourteen and later robbed a bank with other lads. He went to the minors' section of Carabanchel prison for a year. Begonia and Rosi also started taking drugs in their early teens.

I reacted badly to all this. I had been raised in military style—my father was a soldier. I had six brothers and sisters and we lived a very disciplined life, being home by ten o'clock every night. So confronting such disorder in my own home was a terrible experience. I tried to discipline them, but without success. I was faithfully attending the Catholic church and I was also studying the Bible with the Jehovah's Witnesses.

In sheer frustration and desperation I went off to Holland for a while, leaving Rosi, Begonia, Vila and José at home. Two of my other daughters had already moved out. I returned after a month to find the door broken and open, permitting anyone to walk in. Inside I found the floor littered with beer bottles and syringes. The walls were bloodstained from people shooting up. All the doors were damaged and had holes in them. It was just horrific.

I put down my suitcases, surveyed the scene and began to yell at the children. They said the police had broken the doors. I called them and got short shrift. 'They've robbed enough banks, make them pay,' they said.

Meanwhile José was convicted for another robbery and was sent to Burgos prison. I pled with judges, I paid fines up

212

to $5,000 in order to get the boys free, but they just returned to their old ways again. I went off to stay where my other daughters were living, in Gerona. While there I received the awful news that the police had shot and killed José. He had been out looking for drugs. He was armed and very nervous, so when the police approached he got into a shoot-out and was killed. I went back to the others and said, 'How can you put up with this kind of life? Look what you are doing to yourselves—and to me. Nobody should have to put up with this.' And with that I left and never returned for years. I found a job caring for a paralytic man during that time. I left the apartment to the family so that they did not have to live on the streets.

Begonia, with a bunch of fellows, robbed a car. The police turned up and found her in it, so she was sent to prison in Jaén. Rosi joined a gang that robbed a bank. The police caught her and she went to prison in Salamanca. I just seemed to be travelling around the prisons of Spain visiting my family. While all this was going on my parents were paying the rent for our flat.

At one stage I decided to make a plea for the girls. I saw a judge in Jaén and another in Salamanca, and this resulted in the two girls being released.

To show how desperate I was, I tried something new. I took Rosi, Miguel and Begonia away for a holiday in Galicia, but while they were there Miguel decided to rob a bank.

On one occasion I paid for Miguel to go to a sanatorium where they rehabilitate people by giving them sleeping pills. He was there for eight days at a cost of $400, and when he came out he went right back on hard drugs.

Then I met Elliott and Mary Tepper and Lindsay McKenzie. I explained my family situation to them and they told me about a rehabilitation farm where my children could find help. They drove Begonia up to REMAR in Vitoria, but she only stayed a day or two. Then I asked Lindsay to visit Miguel who was still living at home. When Lindsay arrived Miguel said he wanted to go to the centre immediately. Lindsay replied that it would take two weeks to arrange it. Lindsay left, and Miguel lay down on the bed. He began to cry out in a loud voice, 'God, if you are there, help me. Help me, Jesus!' He was crying out so loudly that even the neighbours could hear him. While he was doing this, he says a strange warmth came over him. He got up and ate all the food Lindsay had brought him.

Within an hour Lindsay was back. 'OK, we have arranged a place for you at a centre in Santander. I'll drive you there right now.' So on New Year's Eve the two of them travelled to the RETO centre there.

I was able to visit him six weeks later and he said, 'Mum, I am doing so much better. I believe in God now. All I'm thinking of is being cured myself and helping others.' It was a miracle.

In February, Begonia went to the same place. When she saw her brother she could not believe the change that had come over him. There he was, lifting his hands and praising the Lord!

At Miguel's and Begonia's request I started to attend the Betel church meetings in San Blas. This went on for three years. The two at Santander were doing well, but Rosi was still on drugs. One weekend, when Miguel was with us for a break, we heard someone crying outside the flat. We went out to find Rosi there. We brought her in, made her some coffee, then put her to bed. Next morning Miguel said, 'Are you ready to go to RETO?' She agreed to go. She found the Lord there, but by then she was suffering from AIDS. I visited her before she died, and she just kept telling me, 'Mum, don't worry. If anything happens to me I'll be with the Lord.'

Pilar kept attending church and gradually through the teaching and testimonies of Mary, Elliott, Lindsay, Myk, and others, she started to realise what the Christian life was all about. A feature that really attracted her was the wonderful spirit of worship and praise. She accepted the Lord and after three years was baptised.

She gives a final word about the blessing received through tithing:

Under Elliott's teaching I began to understand a little about the scriptural principle of giving a tenth to the Lord. I started to do this, although I could ill-afford to do so. Some time after I started, my brother died. He had done well in business and was head of a construction firm. I received a share of his estate, so my income actually increased.

Miguel is now a regional leader with RETO and Begonia is married to José Luis, the Spanish president of RETO.

16

THE TAMING OF A WILD IRISHMAN
The story of Noel Ellard

It will be difficult for the reader to visualise the depths to which this wild Irishman, Noel Ellard, sank before he cried out in desperation to God. Living a fast life in South Africa, beaten to the point of death in a Lesotho jail on a murder charge, three times divorced, imprisoned in Greece, mixing with tramps and criminals in France, selling his very life blood for ten dollars a time in Spain, he ended up more dead than alive in Madrid, where two kindly young people introduced him to Betel. He tells his own story:

In 1949 I was born into a lower middle class family in Dublin. These were tough times and my father was hard put to provide for Mother and us five boys. We were brought up in a strongly Catholic environment. I was taught by the Sisters of Mary and later by Jesuits. God, to me then, was a very authoritarian figure as represented by the priests and my father who tended to be very heavy handed.

At an early age I rebelled. I was not impressed by the way Catholicism was working in my country or in my family. There were always rows and fights. My mother was for ever being beaten and we children copped it as well. I remember many a time I was unable to walk because of the beatings received. On Sunday mornings Mum would spend hours in front of the mirror before my father would parade us at Mass. It was a sham.

At sixteen, when the family moved to Birmingham, England, I could not stick it any more, so I left. On the streets

I mixed with bad company and started to drink heavily.

At eighteen I had a relationship with a girl and she became pregnant. I married her and tried to do the decent thing, getting a job and going back to school for some training. It worked for a few years but I still drank heavily and the atmosphere in our home was very oppressive. I came to the point where I could not take it any more.

I realised the children were suffering—we had three by this time—so I left home, left the bank account, and set out on my own. I met another girl with whom I lived for two years and we had a little daughter. But this relationship also broke up.

In 1977 I knew I simply had to settle down, so I enrolled at Northampton Polytechnic for a government-sponsored course that gave me a qualification as a project inspector in civil engineering.

I married again, this time to a Welsh girl of eighteen, and we went, under the Overseas Development Agency, to Lesotho in Southern Africa. But my habits were still the same. I never really cared for anyone but myself—I thought that life revolved around me.

After we had a little boy, my wife said she wanted a divorce because she could not stand living with me any more. 'You are a Jekyll and Hyde. You are nice when you are sober, but when you get drunk I can't get through to you.' So we were divorced amicably.

Culpable homicide

Drink dominated me more than ever after that. I remember driving down to the Lesotho border in a little sports car. It was late at night and, as the border closed at 10.30 pm, I wanted to reach it in time so that I could spend the weekend at the beach, surfing in South Africa. I had been drinking all afternoon and driving too fast. I crashed, the windscreen

217

was smashed, and suddenly I was in the midst of a fearful commotion. A Kalashnikov gun came through the side window and hit me on the head. Two soldiers pulled me out of the car and started to beat me. They said I had killed one of their men. I remember putting my hand in my back pocket to pull out my pass (because I was working on army installations), but they thought I was going for a gun so they cracked a rifle butt over my head. I passed out completely and was taken to jail. I kept passing in and out of consciousness and was repeatedly beaten.

A local white person working for the government heard that another white was in jail (something very unusual in Lesotho) and came to see who it was. It turned out that he was a fellow Free Mason. He moved mountains to have me released, contacting the Irish Embassy, and the Lesotho Prime Minister's office. The Irish Consul general broke his holiday to come and secure my release on the Monday morning. I was a complete mess, beaten black and blue with septicaemia setting in. I almost died.

The government decided to prosecute, and I was on a charge of culpable homicide. The trial dragged on for eleven months and I did not know if I would finish up on the end of a rope or not, because this was a hanging offence. I had been earning big money, but most of it had gone on the divorce settlement. I hired the best lawyer I could afford, but six months into the trial he looked as if he was working for the prosecution, so I had to change lawyers. It came out in court that they thought I was a spy. Eventually the case was dropped because of lack of evidence, but shortly after being released I was attacked by a gang and knifed. Fortunately some people came along and frightened them off, but I realised then that life was too precarious and returned to England.

Mickey Mouse to the rescue

But I could not settle. I had reverse culture shock, and I was now a confirmed alcoholic. I went to live in 'cardboard city' with hoboes and tramps, begging for handouts. I received a cheque from Social Security for £75 and with that I bought a cheap charter flight to Crete (selling the return portion for £50).

I wandered through the islands of the Aegean for three months, living rough on the beaches and doing a bit of fruit-picking. But I was arrested as a vagrant and put in jail. One day the captain pulled his pistol on me and ordered me to sign a document. I didn't know what it was—I could not speak Greek—but I signed it 'Mickey Mouse'. He didn't seem to worry about that, and so I was transferred to another jail in Athens and then led handcuffed to a plane for a flight to London and on to Dublin; but I skipped the connection and stayed in London.

The next time I had some money I went over to Paris and lived a rough life with some punks and gangsters. It was a time of real hardship. I then roamed around France and met up with some fellows who said, 'Come to Spain. There are good pickings there. You can sell your blood.' So I went with three or four others, taking free rides on trains until we were thrown off. We begged for food at the rear of restaurants and when the sun came out we slept on beaches or lived in hovels.

We worked our way from one blood bank to the next. (There were ten of them along the coast.) We received ten dollars each time we gave our 'donation'. If we had a good day and had some money we would buy cocaine or mari-juana. Often I was beaten up. Once my passport was stolen but I found it, soaked through; it had been in the river. I got as far as Madrid and was robbed of everything I had. All I had was the clothing I was wearing. I woke up one cold, cold morning. In the quietness my life passed before me. I knew

I was reaching the end; I was dying. I remember thinking, 'Even if I had money for a phone call, whom could I ring?' I never felt so neglected and rejected. Here I was, 38 years old, and what had I done with my life? Nothing. All I had done was destroy other people's lives. I called out in dejection and desperation, saying, 'Oh God, help me!' And then I thought, 'I don't even believe there is a God.' Well, I thought again and this time I said, 'Well, God, if you are real, please help me. There's no one else left.'

I faded out of consciousness from time to time. I vomited blood and there was blood in my urine, so I knew something was wrong. A man came up and said, 'You need help; I know a place. Come with me and I'll find you help.' He picked me up, threw my arm over his shoulder and half-carried me along some back streets to Misión Urbana, a place of help for street-dwellers and down-and-outs. As I went in I had a distinctly warm impression. The people were so considerate. They didn't preach at me but I sensed the kindness that I had received in France at the Sisters of Mother Theresa.

A young Spanish missionary lass and her English boy-friend were the only two who spoke English. They had to cut off my shoes which were stuck with blood and muck. The fellow went home and brought a pair of his own sneakers for me. I started to cry again. They said, 'Noel, you are in a bad way. We will see what we can do for you.' This place opened only two days a week. I found an old broken-down car not far away and slept in that for a couple of days, then went back the next time the mission opened. During that time they had contacted Betel and arranged to take me to a meeting there.

It was in a pastor's house. There was an Australian there and the others were Spanish. They were a group from the Betel rehabilitation centre. They discussed me with the pastor and it was arranged for me to go with them back to their place after the meeting. I had no baggage, no passport, nothing.

There were fifteen fellows in the house and they just sat with me night and day while I went through the most cruel period of delirium tremens. I saw demons; I felt Satan really laughing at me. There were times when I thought I was at the gates of hell and he was saying, 'I've got you!' But these men prayed over me. I didn't understand their language, but I recognised the love they kept expressing to me night and day. They would fill me up with tortillas, take me for walks, pray with me, and try to keep me from despair. It was a hard couple of weeks, but I realised God was real and that he was answering that desperate prayer. He had reached down into the mire, as it says in Psalm 40, and I knew he was working in my life to bring me out of the mess I was in.

Soon after that I met a New Zealand missionary—Sandra Taylor—and she gave me her Bible. That became my *rock*. I decided that if I could break my old habits, and if God would cure me of these awful cravings, I would commit everything to him. I remember fasting and praying about this and then the warmth that went through me once I had made that total commitment.

A new thrust
The WEC people at Betel kept telling me about their Missionary Training College in Holland which was conducted in English, but I never thought they would accept me in view of my track record. Anyway I applied, and waited. In the meantime Elliott, who had become my mentor, helped me in so many ways. God gave me back my previous musical ability and I began to play the guitar at the worship times. I started to learn Spanish, and my God-given gift of painting came back, so I did all the signwriting for the

centres. All the 'shakes' had gone. After a year I was accepted for training in Holland. Elliott said, 'I will support you in this if you feel it is God's will.'

I had two years in Holland under another Australian, also called Lindsay McKenzie, and the staff there. What a blessed time it was, soaking myself in the word, and learning to communicate the gospel. A whole new world opened up to me. I returned to Spain for my internship year and during that period Elliott proposed that I go to New York to help establish a Betel centre in Brooklyn.

The family

My parents have welcomed me back like a prodigal son. I put my arms round my dad whom I had hated all these years, and was able to say, 'Dad, I love you.' Now my mother writes to tell me that he can't stop talking about me to his friends.

But life is not a bunch of roses. My daughter died last year at twenty years of age. She grew up without knowing the love of her father. I tried over recent years to contact her. I wrote many letters, and she replied. She was at the point of coming to Spain to visit me, but she was invited to a party and took a fatal dose of heroin. It was the first time she had ever injected. I took that to the Lord with bitter tears.

I pray constantly for every one of my four remaining children. The two elder boys from the first marriage are on the streets in England. One of them is a paranoid schizo-phrenic and has been in special homes. A church I am linked with is trying to find him. I write to my children hoping that one day they will see the light and allow the Lord to take charge of their lives.

It is good to know that the Lord will never stop the work he has begun in my life. I am willing to give him everything, to go anywhere, and to do whatever he asks of me.

PAYING THE PRICE

1

THE AIDS NIGHTMARE

by Dr. Renate Kuhl (wife of WEC's International
Secretary, Dr. Dieter Kuhl)

When AIDS was first discovered in the USA in 1981,
nobody expected it to become a global disaster. Only ten
years later it had already taken the lives of hundreds of
thousands of people and by the year 2000 will leave 30-40
million infected and about 10 million children orphaned.

Although recognised in the USA only in 1981, the
causing agent, the Human Immune Deficiency Virus (HIV),
has been present in the world for much longer.

AIDS is not only a disease of homosexuals and drug
addicts; in the developing world vast numbers of people
have been infected by blood transfusions or contaminated
medical instruments. The prevalent transmission mode
world-wide is changing from homosexual to heterosexual.
The risk for women is increasing all over the world, and so
is the risk for babies who are being infected by their mothers
during pregnancy or childbirth.

Dr. Jonathan Mann, director of the Special AIDS Programme of the World Health Organisation and director of
the AIDS Centre at Harvard School of Public Health,
speaks about three stages:

1. The unseen HIV epidemic of the 1970s, when HIV
infected people passed on the virus to others and infection
spread without being recognised. This was possible through
the increase in international travel. By 1981, when the first
cases of AIDS were discovered, approximately 1 million
people were already infected with HIV.

2. The AIDS epidemic of the 1980s, when the number of people suffering from AIDS increased dramatically. In 1987 almost 50,000 world-wide had the disease (most in the USA—45,000). This number grew to over 270,000 by 1990 and to almost half a million (418,403) by October, 1991. Meanwhile the number of those who contracted the virus increased dramatically, reaching the 8 million mark.

3. The AIDS epidemic of the 1990s, with numbers increasing to an estimate of 6 million people suffering with AIDS and 40 million infected with HIV by the year 2000. This decade is characterised by the immense impact of the epidemic on the general public. Society is beginning to see the consequences of this disease in individuals and families, in economic costs and overburdened medical services, as well as in the loss of productive members from society.

Dr. Jonathan Mann says: 'During the next decade HIV will likely reach most communities around the world. Geographic boundaries are no defence. The question is not *if* HIV will come, but *when*.' This year (1993) the number of people carrying the Human Immune Deficiency Virus (HIV) is estimated at 13 million, including over one million children.

It has taken governments a long time to admit that HIV is a problem. After initial denial most countries are now facing up to it and have started national information campaigns and education programmes. But information and education are not enough unless they lead to changes in behaviour patterns. Here churches and missions have a vital role to play.

FACTS AND FIGURES WORLDWIDE

Africa
Africa is the continent most severely affected by AIDS. Famine and civil war have made the situation worse.

Uganda, Tanzania, Zimbabwe and Kenya are at the top of the list. In some Ugandan villages every second person is infected with HIV. It will take about ten more years before the extent of the African AIDS tragedy will be fully revealed. By the year 2000 some African countries will have lost 25% of their active workforce.

The main route of infection is heterosexual intercourse (80%). This puts women at greater risk than in western countries and as a result transmission to children is more likely.

During the current decade several million African babies will contract HIV from their mothers during pregnancy and childbirth. But an even greater number of uninfected children will lose one or both of their parents. In ten countries of Central and East Africa, between 3.1 and 5.5 million children under the age of 15 will be orphaned during the 1990s.

Asia

Compared with Africa numbers were low until 1990, when HIV carriers were just over half a million. However in the coming years, these numbers are expected to grow rapidly, especially in Thailand and India. By AD 2000 Asia will exceed Africa in the number of HIV infections. The main reason for the spread of AIDS in South East Asia is prostitution which is deeply rooted in the culture of some Asian countries. Thousands of women in Thailand and India are sold into prostitution against their own will. Most have no idea of the risk that this entails. Needle sharing among drug users is another major factor in the spread of HIV throughout Asia.

Dr. Jonathan Mann says: 'By 2000 the largest number of infected people will be in Asia—over 40% of the total— followed by Sub-Saharan Africa, then Latin America and the Caribbean.'

In Thailand the number of people testing HIV-positive in 1990 was just 20,700. In 1993 this number has increased to half a million, and by the year 2000 it could be as high as 5 million—10% of the whole population.

In India the first cases of HIV infection were detected among prostitutes in 1986. By 1992 the number had grown to about half a million people. Today (1993) the World Health Organisation estimates that about one million people are infected. AIDS could become the country's biggest public health problem by the turn of the century.

The Western World

In the West absolute numbers are much lower than in Africa or Asia. The USA has an estimated 1 million infected with HIV and just under 250,000 suffering from AIDS, most of whom are men. Since the onset of the epidemic over 150,000 have died.

In Western Europe the total estimated figure of HIV infections is half a million, and about 50,000 are suffering with AIDS. France, Spain and Italy are leading with 150,000, 100,000 and 70,000 HIV-positive people respectively. Generally one can estimate that 10% of these are suffering with AIDS disease already. It is now thought that at least 95% of those infected with the virus will develop symptoms of AIDS.

By the year 2000 Europe is expected to have about 15 million people infected with HIV, and approximately 6 million people suffering with symptoms of AIDS.

Recently there was a clear shift from the homosexual to the heterosexual transmission mode.

In Spain about 65% of all people infected with HIV are intravenous drug users. By 1992, 5,300 people had already died since the onset of the epidemic.

A high percentage of the 1,600 drug addicts who come

into Betel drug rehabilitation centres per year are infected with the AIDS virus. Elliott Tepper wrote in his February, 1990 newsletter: 'More and more of our leaders have begun to wrestle with the first stages of the disease and a majority of the people in our centres carry HIV.'

What does it all mean?
These statistics are not just figures. They are real people and they speak of unbelievable human tragedy. They represent families where grandparents have to care for the children, of teenage children having to fend for themselves and to earn a living for their younger brothers and sisters, of widows who struggle to feed their families and keep going despite feeling unwell. Women are forced into prostitution in order to survive economically. Such statistics speak of the breakdown of whole economies, of collapsing health services, of the ever increasing indebtedness of developing countries to the Western world.

The cost of AIDS cannot be counted merely in terms of medical expenses—although these are enormous and will sooner or later lead to a breakdown of medical services in many countries. The cost must be measured in terms of its impact on the economical and political stability of a country. Here again, developing countries are most affected. As most HIV carriers are between the age of 20 and 40, this will inevitably lead to a decimation of the active workforce (including military) and the future leadership of the community. As a result food production will decrease leading to further economic decline and increase in foreign debts. This will produce more hunger and poverty.

The impact on our world can hardly be imagined. In the near future many African countries will have innumerable orphans who are struggling for survival and whose education will be at risk.

The Aids virus

The virus attacks the human body indirectly, by destroying the body's defence mechanism against infection (immune deficiency). Once the virus has introduced its RNA (Ribonucleic acid) into the genetic material of the T-Lymphocyte it can no longer be eliminated. It will reproduce itself as soon as the body's immune response is activated against any other infection. The newly produced viruses then infect other cells thus eventually destroying the whole immune system. Antibodies against HIV are unable to inactivate the virus. Therefore an HIV carrier is defenceless against infections, especially pneumonia, tuberculosis, herpes and other common infections.

It also directly attacks the Central Nervous System causing brain and nerve damage. This leads to progressive dementia and death. This form of AIDS often shows no antibody response in the blood and is thus less frequently recognised as AIDS.

HIV is transmitted by:

- intimate sexual contact (homosexual or heterosexual). Sexual transmission will become the dominant route in the future, as infected partners will pass it on to one another.

- infected needles and medical instruments, including dental equipment and transfusion of infected blood or blood products. In developing countries contaminated instruments and needles are a common cause of transmission.

- an infected mother to her infant. About 20% of children of HIV-positive parents who test positive after birth will die of AIDS. The rest will lose their antibodies within the first year of life.

HIV is not spread through normal everyday social contact. Hugging, hand-shaking, and the sharing of eating utensils will not pass on the infection. Although very small numbers of the virus have been detected in saliva, sweat and breast milk, the likelihood of transmission by these means is very small and can be ignored.

Aids — presently an incurable disease

A person infected with HIV will develop AIDS within 2-15 years. The majority will develop the disease within 10 years. Initially the victim will look well for many years, but will eventually become increasingly susceptible to infections like pneumonia or tuberculosis. Many suffer from recurring diarrhoea, weight loss, nausea and vomiting. Kaposi sarcoma, a rare form of skin cancer, is frequent in patients with HIV. Once the disease is established it will lead to death within 2-3 years, depending on how long the patient is able to fight off infections.

No cure has yet been found, nor has any vaccine been developed. Scientists are frantically searching for vaccines and drugs. Recently trials of an HIV vaccine have been started in the USA and China on small numbers of volunteers who are at high risk of HIV infection. Much larger numbers would be necessary in these trials to show whether the vaccine actually protects against the virus (*World AIDS Magazine*, September, 1993).

An effective vaccine is probably decades away. Drugs that are available can only help to strengthen the body's immune system or delay the reproduction of the virus, but they cannot eliminate the virus from the body; they are far too expensive for developing countries which can barely cope with the costs of caring for AIDS sufferers. Financial resources for general health in some countries have been completely drained by the demands of AIDS patients. It will not be long before even Western countries come to the limits of their health budget resources.

Therefore it is important that the infection is diagnosed early. This will help a patient receive intensive treatment of any opportunistic infections or other diseases. Thus the life span of a carrier can be prolonged.

Is There Any Hope?

In reading through magazines and listening to reports on TV and radio, one can easily get the impression that mankind is fighting a losing battle. Most countries, after an initial stage of shock and denial, have now come to accept that AIDS is an enormous problem. Can it ever be stopped?

Intensive education and health campaigns, mass distribution of condoms, and other efforts, like legislation against conscious transmission of HIV in some countries, have not achieved much. The number of infections is still growing. Why? Because basic behaviour has not changed. Campaigns advertising condoms as *the* way to prevent HIV infection have only misled people into a false security and meanwhile have encouraged on-going promiscuity.

Governments need the help of non-government organisations in education and prevention programmes, as well as in AIDS care programmes. Here Christians are called upon to face up to the challenge.

Prevention is the only cure for AIDS

AIDS prevention is everybody's responsibility. As the AIDS virus is mainly transmitted by a certain type of behaviour, education to encourage change of behaviour is more strategic than isolation of the infected. Missions and churches can play a vital role in AIDS prevention and education.

Education must include clear information about AIDS and methods of prevention. Two facts are clear:

AIDS is a Fatal Sexually Transmitted Disease. It can be prevented by sexual abstinence before marriage and keeping faithful to one sexual partner for life.

AIDS is a Fatal Disease Transmitted by Blood. It can be prevented by not using or sharing contaminated needles and syringes, and not using unscreened blood transfusions.

Sex education plays a major role in AIDS education. In most countries education campaigns have focused on 'Safer Sex' through the use of condoms. However this has proved to be insufficient and even misleading, as it does not lead to behavioural change. Rather, it encourages promiscuity especially among young people. It has led to a false sense of security. Condoms cannot eliminate the risk of infection. Condoms can only reduce the risk. (The failure rate of condoms in contraception is 5-15%. It is higher for HIV transmission.)

Sex education must promote biblical standards of living. These include having one faithful partner for life, no sex before or outside of marriage, and changing of traditional cultural or ritual customs that put people at risk (e.g. ritual 'cleansing' of widows by sexual intercourse with a relative in some African cultures, or the use of prostitutes, which is a feature of Thai culture).

Uganda and other African countries have accepted the fact that sexual abstinence before marriage and faithfulness within marriage is the only way to contain the epidemic, and this has now become the main emphasis of all their education and prevention programmes.

Problem areas

Since it is predominantly the younger age group that is affected, people at the height of their strength and energy find their hopes and plans suddenly shattered.

Because of the social stigma connected with AIDS, fear, prejudice, rejection, and lack of compassion are evident in many parts of society. Often AIDS victims and their families are isolated and discriminated against. HIV positive people and AIDS sufferers are even rejected by their own families. They become social outcasts.

Families often struggle with the lifestyle of a son or daughter involved in drugs, promiscuity, homosexuality, or criminal offences committed in order to pay for drugs. They often cut off all contact with their son or daughter. They may also have to struggle with legal problems and the complexities of the welfare system.

AIDS leads to misery and prolonged suffering because of many co-existing physical problems. Expensive drugs mean great financial outlay that will inevitably lead to economic hardship. All this may result in a sense of hopelessness. Families struggle with the strain and stress in caring for an AIDS patient at home. It is not easy to come to grips with living in the shadow of death.

It is often difficult to identify the terminal phase of the disease. Very sick patients may improve; others may suddenly die. Usually there is a lengthy dying process. Patients may be unconscious for a week or more. In any case, most people with AIDS want to be involved in their own care and treatment. They want to maintain control of their lives. This helps them to maintain their dignity and a certain quality of life up to the end. Caring for AIDS sufferers calls for the availability of long-term supervisory care and housing. Since there is no cure, the emphasis must be on care.

In addition, people suffering from AIDS struggle with enormous emotional and spiritual problems: self-pity, rejection, grief and bereavement, fear and anger, shattered hopes, isolation, financial hardship, physical suffering and pain, feelings of guilt and shame, and the fear of death.

Therefore there is a great need for a ministry of encouragement and counselling. Ethical questions need to be asked. Should someone who is HIV positive get married to someone who is not? Will he be able to cope with feelings of guilt if he/she sees the partner dying of AIDS? Should couples who are both HIV positive have children? What if the children contract the virus? What about the many orphans and their emotional traumas?

The Christian response to the AIDS disaster
In the midst of tremendous suffering, in the face of a killer disease without a cure, and a frightening situation without hope, the truly Christian community is challenged to find the right response that gives strength and hope and demonstrates loving care and compassion.

The gospel encapsulates answers to many of the problems that the individual, the families of AIDS patients, and whole communities, are facing with regard to AIDS. Here are three lines of action:

- Fear must be dispelled. Normal social contact with people with AIDS is safe and will not lead to infection. Thus the rejection and isolation of people affected by AIDS can be overcome.
- Compassion and love must be demonstrated to those affected by AIDS. Christians who are aware of their own sinfulness and the need of God's grace can communicate God's love to those in need, without being judgmental about their lifestyles.
- We need to be more aware of, and willing to minister to, the deepest needs of people affected by AIDS. This can be done by: listening to their fears and anxieties, coming alongside them in their isolation, being available to help with little things that make life more bearable (shopping, washing, cleaning, baby-sitting). The example of love has an impact on the community. Hopelessness accompanies selfishness; but hope comes where love reigns.

All over the world Christians have become involved in ministering love and hope to individuals, families, and communities affected by AIDS. In Uganda, Zambia, and Tanzania, education and care programmes have been started that can truly be recommended for their impact and success. As in the early centuries when the Christians cared for the victims of the plague, so in our time Christians minister Christ's love and compassion to AIDS victims.

Betel Church faces up to the challenge

The first nationwide Christian Conference on AIDS in Madrid in October, 1992, organised by the leaders of the Betel work, was an unforgettable experience. Over 200 participants from all over the country attended. Church members, workers in drug rehabilitation centres, medical professionals, and a good number of ex-drug addicts came together to testify to THE OTHER FACE OF AIDS (the conference theme).

My husband and I were invited as speakers. Our task was to give information on AIDS and its impact on the world and highlight its challenge to the Christian community. We found deep interest and attention from the audience on this hot issue.

Throughout the day we had very lively discussion sessions. But most of all, we were deeply touched by the testimonies of a dozen people with AIDS as they shared how they live and cope with their situation. Most of them were still young. Most had been infected through intravenous drug use. Some had contracted the virus from their spouse. Some were living with a very low T-cell count (a measure for the body's level of defence against infections). Humanly speaking they should no longer have been alive. However they were living as a bright testimony of the Lord's miraculous power and grace. All were bright Christians radiating the joy of the Lord and completely committed to using the years left to them to minister to other drug addicts.

This was the other face of AIDS. There was hope and joy. There was determination. There was vision and strength. There was the willingness to be committed, to bring love and hope to those in darkness, and to declare that there is more to life than what can be seen.

These ex-drug addicts were all members of a loving community, the Betel Church. They knew where they belonged. They had a home, and they knew that they would not be isolated but cared for in the hard times to come, and that this was not the end.

A call to intercession

As the global impact of the AIDS disaster becomes clear, Christians from all around the world are called not only to action, but also to intercession. Bishop Misaeri Kauma of Namirembe Diocese in Kampala, Uganda wrote this prayer:

> Almighty God, our Heavenly Father, who enabled your servant Job to go victoriously through great bodily suffering, without denying your name, power and love, have mercy on us, Lord, who are stricken by this epidemic of AIDS.
>
> Stretch out your healing hand and hold back the virus.
>
> Strengthen and comfort, in Jesus Christ, those infected, and ease their pain of body and mind.
>
> Send your Holy Spirit to renew us all, and lead us into repentance and faith in the gospel.
>
> Give us the gift of discipline, that we may keep our bodies and minds clean and holy.
>
> Grant wisdom and knowledge and perseverance

to all who seek a cure for AIDS, that they may find the drugs to prevent and heal AIDS.

Have mercy on us, Lord and on all AIDS sufferers throughout the world.

Give love and compassion to all who seek to assist them, through Jesus Christ, our Lord. Amen.

2

THE COST
by Elliott Tepper

Once you start to take care of drug addicts and bring them under your roof, it becomes a costly exercise. Try to imagine approximately 700 men and women and their children living under your roof and having to be fed, clothed and sheltered. At this point in time we have over 90 properties in 18 provinces of Spain, in New York City, in North Africa and in Naples, Italy. That costs money. So does transportation. We have a fleet of approximately one hundred vehicles—vans, trucks and cars. Try to calculate the cost of purchasing them, insuring them and then gasoline and diesel fuel to keep them running. It's expensive. In that very practical sense, it's costly.

Sacrifice is involved
Then, there's the cost of taking care of our people within the programme. When addicts arrive, they go through the withdrawal syndrome. We don't allow them to take any drugs; they go 'cold turkey'—no tranquillisers, no substitute opiates like methadone—total abstinence.

The new addicts have a hard time. Some of them don't sleep for a week, some for a month: they're anxious, and the people who have to live with them, the cured addicts, often have to sacrifice sleep. They must be prepared to talk to them at all hours, take them on walks, give them massages, and encourage them to persevere. Day after day, week after week, this programme continues, and it is costly. Many missionaries romanticise about working and living with drug addicts, but after a week in a residence the romanticism evaporates and the reality of their call and the quality of their love are truly tested.

In a typical centre, we have a 'watch' every night; at least one person will stay up for an hour at a time so there's always someone awake, usually with the light on, with the fire burning if it's cold. That means that those who are passing through withdrawal have someone to talk to; they don't feel alone. And it lets them know that someone cares for them, will be with them and love them. That's costly.

I think we should also acknowledge the great contribution that Lindsay McKenzie made to Betel. When we started I already had my wife and family, so the drug addicts couldn't live with Mary and me and the four boys in our small apartment. But Lindsay was a single worker then. He opened his home and stayed up all night with Raúl, Pino and the other men. Lindsay was the first one to carry that load and that's to his eternal credit.

Twentieth century lepers

Another cost would be the social stigma of working with drug addicts. Drug addicts are the twentieth century's lepers.

Nobody in society wants drug addicts near them. No one wants to have a drug centre in the neighbourhood, and certainly not in the same building. Even recently, when we were talking to the bureaucrat in charge of the Social Programme for the Regional Plan Against Drug Abuse in the Province of Madrid, she told me that we would be required to have individual licences for each of our centres. Up until now, the government hasn't really demanded that from us; but with the new 1991 law, they're trying to bring all the social action groups under one register. I said, 'But how can we do that?' She said, 'Just do the major buildings;

don't worry about your smaller places: we don't even have licences for our government properties. The local authorities won't even give us licences because none of the neighbours will sign agreements allowing them to be there.' The government functions without a licence. It's a double standard—to demand a licence from us when they don't have a licence for themselves.

Prejudice

Included in the social stigma is class prejudice. Spaniards are very class conscious. The way you speak, the way you dress, your education, your job, where you live—these all classify you. Spaniards are very proud. To their credit, this pride makes them a clean, neat and orderly nation, but they are a very aggressive society. It is no accident that they conquered half the world. Low class drug addicts just simply don't make it. People don't want anything to do with them. Drug addicts are thieves and criminals generally. They have to steal from society to maintain their habit. Sometimes they steal up to $500 or $1000 a day. They are like a plague of locusts that descends on society. Little by little they begin to lose their health and their beauty. Their bodies become scarred from the needle marks; their general self-respect and self-esteem drops; they don't take care of themselves; they don't shower or wash. This kind of behaviour and conduct is very un-Spanish.

Once they really are down and out, they are rejected by their family; and since they can no longer maintain a home, they begin to live on the street and drift from one old house to another, from one old car to another. They are dirty, filthy, and are very unlovely. So naturally they are rejected. Also they are sick. People don't want to be with them because they are afraid of AIDS and of contagious diseases like hepatitis, pneumonia or tuberculosis. We who work with them are not afraid of AIDS; we're more concerned about hepatitis, viral pneumonia and viral tuberculosis. There are strains coming through them which are very deadly. Hepatitis B and C can kill you. To our knowledge none of our workers has contracted these deadly diseases—with the exception of one ex-addict who married a missionary.

We have wonderful worship at Betel. There's good preaching and teaching, so people are inspired and encouraged. They like to be in our meetings, but many won't join our church because they don't want to be too closely identified with a twentieth century 'leper colony', and they certainly don't want their sons and daughters falling in love with ex-drug addicts—even if they are cured and full of the Holy Spirit. They are afraid, in short, of contracting AIDS.

Inner city life

Another cost, for me, is the fact that drug addicts come from the city. Therefore, we must locate in their domain. Having to live in the inner city is a sacrifice for me. My wife comes from beautiful Wilmington, North Carolina, the azalea capital of the world, a lovely southern port city with trees, flowers, lots of clean air and beautiful white sand beaches. I come from Long Island, New York, from the wealthy suburbs on the south shore. I grew up in clean air with green trees and gardens. Now we live in Madrid, a lovely, historic city of four million people. But, although there are parks and quiet areas, it is one of the most contaminated cities in Europe, with air pollution and heavy traffic. And of course we work with people who live in the poorer parts of the city. That's not easy. My boys have not grown up in the same kind of neighbourhood as I did. If they want some sport they have to play soccer in the street or on a dirt lot. As a parent I would like them to know the same natural beauty familiar to me as I grew up. But God knows. He has given them the recompense of an inner spiritual life that I never knew as a child. And besides, time is very short, and eternity without end.

Emotional and personal costs

There is the high emotional cost of constantly losing beloved workers who succumb to AIDS. They have a shortened life span. You work with people who will die prematurely. I've probably attended more funerals than any other pastor in Spain, with the exception of maybe the Pollnows and Miguel Diez. At RETO, REMAR and Betel we are always having to bury the people we love.

I remember being in a meeting in Madrid with about twenty of the principal city pastors and they were talking about problems. One of them asked: 'I have this person attending my church and he has the AIDS virus. What do I do? It is a crisis!' I said, 'It is all relative. We have three quarters of our church with the AIDS virus.' We just have to live with that. It breaks your heart when they die. You form bridges, you form friendships and then they're broken. We live in the shadow of death. But most of them die in the Lord.

Also it's costly for my wife and family. Now that the work has spread to eighteen provinces and to America, North Africa and Italy, I have to keep moving around, and so I'm separated from them for an average of two and a half days a week. I recognise my priorities: God, my wife, my children, and the work of the Lord, and I certainly don't want to win the world and lose my family. But by the grace of God we've been able to communicate the love of God and our faith to our children. All our boys know God, and that's because of the strength and many virtues of my good and godly wife, Mary, and my commitment to the family. I could travel all over the country more. I could go to foreign conferences even more; but I've decided to build my family in Madrid, to stay close to them, to build the church where I am, and discipline myself just to give the minimum time to the outward extension of the work. Nevertheless, that time is two and a half days a week. I have to be away for that period.

In the last five years I've put 250,000 kilometres on my van visiting our work in Spain. That doesn't count all the plane flights and other trips here and there. And the two and a half days a week doesn't count the extended two and three week trips that I've had to make at times.

3

ADAPTABILITY — THE CHALLENGE FOR
OVERSEAS WORKERS

*Workers from many countries play a significant role in the
total Betel operation, and all have to face their own particu-
lar cross-cultural hurdles. Some find it easier than others.
Problems of length prohibit detailed mention of people like
Sandra Bautista from New Zealand, Graham and Sue
Single from Australia and New Zealand, and Kent and Mary
Alice Martin from the United States. However here are the
stories of just four.*

*Because of Elliott's close links with Mexico a warm support-
ive relationship exists between the Amistad churches there
and Betel. A number of missionaries have made a significant
contribution to the work. Raúl Reyes explains his position:*

I am a member of the Amistad de Puebla church in Mexico.
I left university to attend the church Bible School for two
and a half years, then the church fellowship agreed to send
me to Betel. My greatest joy is the acceptance I have had
with the Spaniards over the past three and a half years.

My service covers many areas. I lead worship at the
Mejorada centre and take morning devotions at several
centres. I teach the children at the main church, and take my
share of leading evangelistic outreach on the streets and in
the parks. I also conduct a Bible study group in Fuenlabrada.
I feel very fulfilled and have lots to do, although some
aspects of life here are not so easy. For instance, I work
closely with those going through rehabilitation, living with

them and discipling them for perhaps several months. It is very discouraging when suddenly some of them leave. Yet, I see God powerfully at work in others, so I go on.

I have been able to return to Mexico several times and I have found that my testimony has made quite an impact on my home church and other churches in the Amistad group. I have been able to speak at a large missionary convention of a thousand people and bring the work of Betel before them.

Every year I have been here things have changed for the better, and I do believe that God means to pour out his Spirit on this land.

One from a totally different background is Bian Tan who was born in Malaysia, is now an Australian citizen and has been sent out from there. Here is her story.

I grew up in a mixture of Chinese and Malaysian cultures. My parents were not Christians, so I tried all sorts of beliefs —Buddhism, Islam, Kungfu, Yoga, and so on, but my life was still empty.

My younger brother heard the gospel and his life was changed. I saw God's love in him and I realised that I needed what he had. One night I decided to give my life to Christ and from then he has been my Saviour.

I studied for two years in the Bible College of Queensland and then applied to WEC in Australia for overseas service. The day finally came when I arrived in a cold wintry Madrid. I had very little Spanish and had dreadful culture shock.

Eventually the Mission agreed that I should serve with Betel, and the moment I walked into the girls' residence in Valencia, I knew that this was the place where God wanted me. I still feel like that, three years later.

In the beginning I had lots of difficulties. I had to share

246

a clothes closet with two other inmates. I had a bed in a dormitory along with seven other girls and two children. Every night one of the children, a two-year old, would cry and cry. It was a good thing I was a solid sleeper. There was no privacy or quietness, and this made it hard to spend time with God, but as time went on I seemed to get over these problems.

Many of the girls were curious to know why a Chinese 'drug addict' had to come all the way to Spain to be cured! I hardly spoke a word, but kept working with them, doing the tasks that they were doing. I guess I even looked like an addict because I was all skin and bone. Some did not know I was a missionary.

After being here long enough to understand how addicts behave, I was given the responsibility of being a 'shadow' to a new girl. The job entailed staying with the other person every hour of the day.

Many a time I have felt like packing my bag and leaving. I remember looking after a girl day in and day out for nearly a year. I was eager—perhaps too eager—to see her converted. She went along OK and then suddenly just turned against me. 'You're pushing me! Back off!' I felt like screaming, but the Lord said, 'This is *my* work, not yours.'

I remember one day we had a pastoral visit from our field leader. He asked me, 'What do you feel is your main ministry here?' I did not really know how to reply, so I just said one word, 'Serving.'

I think one fault I have is trying to get the girls converted too quickly. The Lord keeps reminding me, 'Bian, be patient; you know who I am.' Life in this centre is not easy; it is full of problems, but I keep reminding myself that 'the prayer of a righteous man (woman) is powerful and effective.'

I am not an 'up front' person. But one thing I know: God has given me the ability to love people and enjoy both

247

listening and talking to them. God has put a compassion in my heart.

This is a fruitful ministry. Fellows and girls are being touched by the Lord. It is marvellous to see them grow spiritually and then become leaders in the work, able to teach others. It is a joy to see God's hand on their lives. I have had the privilege of seeing sons and daughters restored to their parents; I have seen marriages reborn and love come back into them.

For fruit to come it really is necessary to live with these people. That shows you want to identify with them. I realise it is not feasible for married staff people to do it; but I can do it. Most of these addicts come from broken homes; their self-esteem is low; they have inferiority complexes. Many girls say to me: 'We know that you care, and that you love us. We see you not as a missionary but as a friend. You are one of us.'

These last three years have been the happiest in my life.

Armando has been working with Betel for several years and is a gifted and much valued worker. Here is his story.

I came from Mexico to Spain in May 1988 with the idea of working with Elliott Tepper in *Centro Betel*. I knew very little about drug addicts, but that didn't matter. What mattered was the call of God to come to Spain.

For the first weeks I lived with the men in the Barajas house, but soon came the forced change to the centre in Mejorada del Campo. I was asked to join the first team that had to fix up the house. It was quite an odyssey. The house was in ruins, with hundreds of spiders and insects everywhere. Before it was ready, the rest of the men arrived. There was no electricity, no water, no toilets. We had to bathe in the river and with well water. For me this was a time of testing. Two things helped me: prayer and faith that God would work wonders in the lives of the drug addicts.

My objectives among them were to sow the word day after day, and to encourage praise and worship. Soon the transforming presence of the Holy Spirit could be felt. I began to see significant changes in many of the men.

It was awesome to discover the ravages that heroin made in young lives. Physically, they seemed to arrive like garbage blown in by the wind, like old people ending their days. They were the dregs of society, very insecure and full of hurts.

I lived like one of them, working, eating, relating to them, and sleeping in the same house. I had to clean up the vomit of someone going through withdrawal, encourage the depressed ones, or minister deliverance to the demonised.

I remember when Javi arrived with his beard and long dirty hair full of lice, his face covered with scabs, and his body like a skeleton. On the first night he slept in the bunk bed below me and the lice climbed up into my bed. I had to wash him, cut his hair and lovingly care for him.

In a few weeks he received Christ as Lord and Saviour and took firm hold of the word. Now he leads worship, and pastors the centre and church in Cuenca.

The number of men and women kept growing and new centres opened. It became necessary to give some basic, yet solid instruction in order to sustain spiritual growth. In our hearts was born the idea of a Bible Institute to equip those who had a calling to serve the Lord. The Adullam Bible Institute began in January, 1989. The students received not only theological instruction, but instruction in character and discipline as well. Although the institute is small, I can say that after five years it has helped to produce nine pastors and twenty-one missionary workers serving in Spain, New York and Naples.

After nearly six years I continue to serve with Betel. I'm

now the director of the Adullam Bible Institute, but have other responsibilities also.

I was recently married to Emma, a beautiful Mexican woman who shares the same missionary vision. Together we want to serve God in this country and minister to these people whom the world has discarded, but who are a special treasure loved by God.

Irene Wood

'Take my strength,' the Lord said to me as I approached my field leader's door. This only partly prepared me for the shock of hearing that I was to enter Betel the following week. I had thought that, like most new WEC missionaries, I would be going on some summer outreach campaign.

Friday evening came and I arrived with my few things to be admitted to the drug centre. Carmen was to be my house leader. I felt really apprehensive as I walked into the courtyard. 'Hola,' Carmen said with a lovely toothless grin. She was perhaps as tall as my chest and had long curly hair. She was to be a great help to me over the next few months.

I lived in the 'Chalet' in a small town outside Madrid where I spent many long days sewing string baskets and listening to the girls. A lot of what was said went over my head as I had only completed one basic four-month language course and had shared a flat with other missionaries. My language skills were very limited. There were many others lessons to learn as I lived the life of a 'Betelita'.

The cultural differences were great. I had determined not to complain or be a bother, but rather to submit to whatever came my way each day.

It was one of the happiest times of my life.

Carmen was able to travel with some others to England to have dental treatment and returned with a beautiful white smile. What a joy!

Trini, the second in charge, took me under her wing. They were all very kind to me. I knew how hard it must have been to have someone with them always who could not communicate well, and how much patience it required to listen.

Each girl became very important to me. I was excited to see growth and so sad to see others leave, often after a reasonable length of time. It seemed they were losing so much by leaving.

During my time with the girls I sensed the Lord's call to stay with Betel, which is what I did following the completion of my language study and six months with a church planting team in Cuenca.

I became the Betel nurse. This involved liaising with the Infectious Disease team at a leading Madrid hospital. I attended to out-patients, observing and studying their AIDS-virus treatment and clinical progress. This helped keep me current with the latest treatments so that Betel's leadership could offer informed counsel to those who were facing some very big decisions in their lives.

I think knowing and supporting Marimar (see Section 2, chapter 3) through her illness has been my most poignant experience in Betel. Much could be said of Marimar and how endearing she was to everyone, but my special memory is of her desire to serve the Lord even while she lay sick in the hospital. She did just that, as those who visited her can recall. I would go there wishing there was some comfort I could bring her, often wondering just what I could say this time. Each visit was unique. Sometimes we would sing, other times just chat, but always I left impressed by her love of God and desire for his presence. It is not easy to support a dying friend. Many complex issues surround the death of a young mother whose desire is to serve the Lord wholeheartedly. There are no easy answers, if any at all. What I've seen in Marimar and many others is an abandonment to

Christ and a faith in his love and power that survives the very real fears, pain and doubts.

'Take my strength' was not just a word of encouragement for an unexpected change of plans, but a promise of that strength in all that was to come, one of the most precious times of my life.

4

TRANSFORMED LIVES MAKE IT ALL WORTHWHILE
An interview with Lindsay and Myk McKenzie

While the results of Betel's ministry are spectacular, it is not without a high cost in terms of human commitment. The trauma and stress that missionaries and national workers experience—as well as the huge workload they carry— exact a heavy toll in their personal lives.

Most of the questions put to Lindsay and Myk in this chapter are designed to obtain details of what is involved in running a rehabilitation centre.

Amy Carmichael has written movingly about this principle of 'life out of death':

There is no gain but by a loss,
We cannot save, but by the Cross;
The corn of wheat to multiply,
Must fall into the ground and die.
O, should a soul alone remain,
When it a hundredfold can gain?

Our souls are held by all they hold;
Slaves still are slaves in chains of gold;
To whatsoever we may cling,
We make it a soul-changing thing,
Whether it be a life or land,
And dear as our right eye or hand.

Whenever you ripe fields behold,
Waving to God their sheaves of gold,
Be sure some corn of wheat has died,
Some saintly soul been crucified.
Someone has suffered, wept, and prayed
And fought hell's legions undismayed.

Is work in a drug rehabilitation centre demanding?
Lindsay: Yes, it is demanding because we are on call 24 hours a day. There is very little time for normal family life, and yet the family becomes part of the total picture. But it is all so very worthwhile. We just need to keep working at finding the right balance.

It's demanding because each arrival has many complications that need to be sorted through. Many have deep hurts that need to be addressed, and we often have to make representation before judges and prison authorities on behalf of those who join us. We also have to struggle with red tape. It is a truly superhuman feat coping with the regulations; in fact, if we waited for official permission for everything, we would get nothing done. The authorities demand so many square metres of space for each person; a toilet for so many people, and so on.

Yes, work here is stressful; we are often on edge because we are involved with people who are unpredictable. New emergencies are always cropping up.

Are you fulfilled?
Lindsay: When lives are radically changed it just makes up for everything. We know what these young people have been doing, the hurts they and their families have suffered, and what they have done to society. Then we see them start to walk normally and to take an interest in others. The contrast is just mind-boggling. It's a complete transformation.

It's people that count. When a person comes through for God and goes on spiritually, you know that he is going to touch a great many people: his family, his contacts, others who rub shoulders with him in the centres. Many of them stay on with us and serve the others who come in, as well as reaching out to those still on the streets.

The demanding role we had at the start (helping new arrivals through the withdrawal period) we have handed on to others, and we concentrate now on the training and pastoring of future leaders. The fulfilment in that is fantastic.

Not one day goes by without our thanking God for bringing us into this work. We just love it. The fulfilment aspect far outweighs the pressures and demands. In fact, we don't often think of it in terms of 'demand'. God has called us and he gives us the buoyancy that carries us through.

Mind you, there's no kind of start or finish to a day. The routine is ragged. One morning I can start at five or six o'clock and by 10 am I might go home to see the family. Another time I may not see them all day and still be working late into the night. Each day is so completely different; you can plan carefully, but it seldom works out as expected.

What are the pluses in all this?
Myk: I think one of our greatest joys is the fact that we see fruit very early. We admire others who slog away and wait for years for a harvest. We are fortunate because we have a key into society at the moment. Drugs are a huge problem and we have the answer.

Another plus is that we *love* what we are doing! As a young Christian nurse I always dreamed of being involved in something which met the combined physical, emotional and spiritual needs of people, and this is what we are doing.

Lindsay: People see us as doing a credible task. We are not seen as 'weirdos' just handing out tracts. People relax with us and we can talk very naturally to them. They don't feel they are targets of missionaries, yet they are!

The gospel is lived out and intensive discipleship training goes on all the time. It is not a theoretical idea—they *see* the gospel even before they understand it, and it breaks down barriers when they sense the love of Jesus being shown to them. When they come to the meetings and hear a sermon or attend a Bible study, their curiosity has already been awakened and they want to know why we live as we do.

Myk: When we represent the centre before legal bodies and judges we are doing something important in the social system, because there is such need in this area. Everyone recognises the immensity of the drug problem and they are glad to find a group that will take on addicts, particularly those who are HIV positive. (Mind you, there are also those who would like to see every Christian centre shut down!)

Lindsay: One of our greatest joys is seeing marriages restored and families re-united. We help couples who have been separated for years and are thinking of divorce. We become involved in custody cases where previously there has been no hope of having the children back from being wards of the state. But lives are changed and we can testify before the authorities to that fact, and they listen to us.

We listen to our folks' testimonies and marvel at the power of God which transforms people. Sometimes when I hear the sordid events in their past I feel like saying, 'Stop! I don't want to hear any more; it's so repugnant. I don't want to see you in that light.' But it is then you realise the depths to which the Lord has gone to save them.

Many a time I've said to one of the fellows after hearing his testimony, 'Look, I just can't believe that you did those things. Seeing you now, how you love God, how you maintain a holy walk—it's just as if you're talking about somebody else.'

Myk: I think the title of this book, and C. T. Studd's poem from which it is taken, sums up our sentiments correctly:

> Some people wish to live within
> the sound of church or chapel bell,
> I'd rather run a rescue shop
> within a yard of hell.

We relish our calling and feel spoilt in that we enjoy our work so much, although, of course, there are times of great disappointment too. But the former far outweighs the latter.

What are the negatives? What kind of disappointment do you experience?

Lindsay: We have just had a recent case of a fellow who came to us three years ago and perhaps for him more than any other, we've really stuck our necks out in courtrooms, with the police, and with the prison authorities, because we saw potential in him.

He seemed to want to go through with God. It paid off and God did a miracle by causing the prison authorities to look favourably on him. He was allowed to start a seven year sentence at our centre instead of jail. Now we have discovered that he really does not want anything to do with God, and we are back to square one. That kind of thing leaves you totally deflated, until your eyes are back on the Lord again. Of course, if he leaves the program and goes out on the street again, it means we have to go back to the authorities and be open with them.

Sometimes one can become quite callous, and it is at that

point that God needs to renew in us that fresh hope for each newcomer, even though we know that the majority are not going to make it. It's so easy to judge a new arrival and say, 'This fellow won't stay long.' Often that is the very one who goes ahead! We see others and we think, 'Wow! This person seems hungry for God. He'll go places.' And that's the one who doesn't. Nowadays we are trying not to pre-judge.

We have some very practical problems too. Because of our financial limitations, vehicles are generally old and unreliable. This is a constant problem, as transport is vital to the smooth running of a centre.

Also, regulations are very demanding for groups like ourselves with no government funding. We offer the best services we can under the circumstances, but are frequently threatened with closure because we do not have private doctors and psychologists and hospital standard facilities. REMAR, RETO and Betel (three of the largest evangelical centres in Spain) house and care for thousands of men, women and children, without charge, but are still regarded as 'sects' and ignored in official statistics.

Myk: Our biggest heartache is that although many hundreds come through our centres each year, most do not stay long enough to have a total cure. Some return several times. Our record in Valencia is seven admissions for the same person. It breaks our hearts to see a desperate man or woman leave, only to fall further into addiction, land up in prison, or even die through an overdose, violence or AIDS.

Does it get any easier?
Myk: It gets easier in the sense that we know how to deal with routine situations and we have the facilities to take in needy persons, provided they accept the conditions of entry.

We are not 'conned' so easily now! In the early days we were so 'green', we didn't realise that they were lying to us. They came with such pleading and with such tears that we believed them, or felt obliged to believe them. Now most of the new arrivals are screened by our leaders who are themselves rehabilitated ex-addicts and who know every trick in the book, so they are rarely deceived.

Lindsay: Learning to delegate has helped to take the pressure off. We take many risks by putting new Christians into positions of responsibility, mainly because there is no other option. Sometimes they fail and that is disappointing. It's a risk. They can make mistakes; they feel threatened; they're not always wise. A lot of immature decisions are made about other people's lives that horrify us. People have left because a leader has made a harsh or unloving decision, or taken a dislike towards someone. That weighs heavily upon us.

What makes it worthwhile?
Myk: Seeing broken people made whole. Seeing children re-united with their mums and dads and learning the ways of the Lord Jesus. Seeing husbands and wives coming together after having been separated for years. We have one such couple at the moment. They are re-united with their little girl.

Another couple were completely separated. (She was even living with another man.) Now they have come back together. It's almost as if they're on their second honeymoon, yet he's slowly succumbing to AIDS. It's so special when you see how God does this, and gives them heaven on earth.

Lindsay: In a nutshell what makes it worthwhile is seeing Jesus reproduced in lost and destroyed lives, seeing the overcoming power of Jesus and seeing Satan kicked out!

You see a devil changed into a saint and a prostitute turned into a pure woman. It's beautiful, a hardened violent man becomes a gentleman and a man of God. That's what makes it worthwhile.

We have seen homosexuals delivered—not many, but some. One man is now happily married and has children. He is totally transformed. Another is now a leader. God has washed away the shame of all that he has gone through as a young man. He is now in the business of helping others find that same freedom.

How do you handle the AIDS issue?

Lindsay: It is hard to accept that a person whom we have come to know and love is in the terminal stage of AIDS. It might just suddenly come on, and then we know this life will soon be cut short. We see people grappling with these issues as they are wasting away. God has placed us here to be sentinels for them on their way to death.

It's a privilege to attend these AIDS sufferers; they have a unique outlook on life and they give us a fresh awareness of eternity as they keep their eyes on heaven. AIDS is an awful, wasting disease and it really tears at one's heart when God finally takes them. We have learned so much from these dear people. Someone said recently that AIDS sufferers live enhanced lives. That sounds strange, but it's true. They enter into a new dimension of living that others can never appreciate.

Myk: One of our girls, Milagros, died of AIDS last year. She had lived on the streets all her life and had been in prison seven times, the final sentence being seven years for armed robbery. Just a few days before it happened one of our girls, Yolanda, was with her, caring for her. Milagros began groping with her arms; she could hardly speak because she was dying of an HIV complication—a sarcoma of the tongue and larynx. She was actually suffocating from this massive tumour growing in her throat and mouth. She had great difficulty in breathing and was on medication, but she saw Jesus. Yolanda, who was beside her, saw her struggles and was weeping, but Milagros turned to her with a look of immense satisfaction and said, 'Why are you weeping? Don't cry. It's Jesus. I can see him. Isn't he beautiful? Isn't he handsome? He's coming to take me.' From that moment Yolanda was a changed person. She was finally convinced about the reality of Christ and is now growing in grace.

I remember quite a few visits to Marimar, one of our dear friends who died leaving a husband and two little girls. Each visit was heartbreaking but there was something so special; it was almost as though heaven was in the room with you. There was something different about her. The presence of God was so real and she could talk about death. At times she was very positive, at times she wept on my shoulder, crying over leaving her husband and two little girls. I never visited without weeping myself.

Can you give an outline of your methods?

When addicts come into the centre they go through 15 to 30 days of withdrawal symptoms—'cold turkey', that is, without any medical help. Other inmates are assigned to help them and encourage them. Each one is accompanied by a monitor or 'shadow'—someone who has been a drug addict but is doing well and has been given responsibility. We always send them out in twos.

Families naturally want to visit, so we say to them, 'The visiting hours are the church meeting times.' That forces the family to come along to a church meeting and hear the gospel!

We do all sorts of jobs, and this is a good thing because

261

they're going to have to work when they leave. At the same time this provides an income for the centre. If money comes in, it is put into a common pool and that pays the expenses of their stay with us.

The main thing is that in all this activity they see the gospel lived out. They can see how leaders react when things go well or when tragedy strikes, or when funds are short. They see how we behave as married couples. All this takes place in a community atmosphere, and the reality of the gospel is lived out in a very practical way. All the monitors are ex-drug addicts. When new arrivals realise that these workers have been where they've been, then their words carry a lot of weight.

Is it not hard and legalistic to require 'cold turkey' treatment? To prohibit smoking and not allow any boy/girl relationships?

Myk: Yes, it is a bit cold and legalistic, but it is the shortest route. We found that the best and quickest way is just to state our requirements. Then there are no problems; there's no fighting or black-marketing. We don't allow tobacco, alcohol or pills. Most come to us having taken every drug available—tranquillisers, cocaine, heroin (sniffing and mainlining), alcohol, etc. Some even drank cologne or pure alcohol, straight or mixed with a coke or other beverage.

It's best for them to go 'cold turkey' and have the poison cleaned out of their systems. Admittedly they don't sleep for two to four weeks and it's a painful time. They feel as if they are having a massive dose of the 'flu. They can be nauseated; they can vomit; they can be angry and frustrated. But someone is with them all the time to talk to them, encourage them, take them for a walk, give them a shower —anything to help them through.

After the physical withdrawal syndrome comes the

psychological. They can feel and dream that they are shooting up and the urge to return to heroin is overwhelming.

We take a firm line, too, about friendships. We allow these only after eighteen months in the centre. That gives them time to decide whether they are going to go on with God or not. If they do, then they are likely to make a good decision regarding a life partner.

Lindsay: Because addicts have lived in so much immorality and promiscuity, we have to be radical. There are no half measures. They appreciate black and white concepts. Because of this, they face the idea of total discipleship right from the start. We don't encourage our folk to make decisions without understanding that this means discipleship. It's total commitment or nothing, and they know that.

Myk: Heroin addicts don't have much desire for food and generally come to us undernourished. Sexual desire is minimal. But when they come off the drug their bodily appetites are awakened as if from a deep sleep. They eat voraciously and the sex drive becomes very strong, so we have our work cut out helping them in these areas and have to be strict. The men like to play soccer, and we give them heavy manual work like loading and unloading trucks to absorb their energy.

How is the work financed?
Lindsay: 95% of the income of the centre comes from finance generated by the work that the men and women do. Now and again we get a gift from churches overseas, but that is a very small percentage of the income. We don't have any government help whatsoever.

How do you counsel someone who has AIDS and wants to marry someone who hasn't?

Lindsay: It's a very controversial question. It's not one to which a person can give a black or white answer. I would say that each case is different. We don't have pat answers. Our job is to make sure that both parties fully understand all the physical and medical aspects.

People are shocked that we would marry a couple when one party has AIDS, but we've discovered that if we say 'no' then they go out and marry anyway. If they are going to be married they might as well have the blessing and the support of the church family. Our responsibility is to make sure that they are well informed.

Myk: We are very specific. We explain that the non-infected party will eventually contract the disease. We tell them that any children born to them will probably be HIV positive, with the possibility of 20% of them developing AIDS. We talk about the likelihood of the children becoming orphans one day.

They have to face taking the marriage vows—'in sickness and in health, till death us do part'—but once they have made their decision then we stand with them through the difficult times ahead.

Lindsay: When people say that it's wrong for them to marry because of the suffering that will come, we say that avoiding suffering is not necessarily the highest goal. There's a law of love that's higher and greater.

If people want to leave the centre, do you try to stop them?

Lindsay: No. If we hear that someone is packing and intending to leave we move alongside and gently ask, 'Do you really know what you are doing? Do you know what you are heading for? Do you realise you are throwing everything overboard?' It depends very much on the person. Frankly, we are sometimes glad when a person chooses to leave, if there have been big problems. Sometimes we actually take the initiative and ask people to go. Perhaps we say, 'Look, this isn't working out. Why don't you go home for a week or two and think about it? If you do decide to return I think we'll need to see a stronger motivation in you.' We don't try to stop them in a physical way. That's against the law for a start, and secondly we don't want to have such people in the centre because they just cause problems.

What is the procedure for new arrivals?

Myk: We like to have new enquirers visit us beforehand if at all possible. If not we talk to them by phone. It's at this point we explain the rules: no smoking, no drinking, no drugs. We point out that this is a Christian centre so they will receive teaching from the Bible.

When they arrive they come to the office and their personal particulars are taken down: name, address, parents, type of addiction, and so on. Everything is checked, down to the clothes they are wearing. They are asked to take a shower and then they are taken to the men's or women's residence where they are welcomed, and settled in.

It's incredible to see what people bring—pills or heroin in the lining of their jeans or the hems or waistband; women hide drugs in their vagina, men in their anus; they sew it into the sides of bags. All sorts of things. They will do anything to help themselves through withdrawal. They are terrified of 'cold turkey', so we spend a lot of time trying to calm them.

The first day or so they're high because they've usually shot up or smoked a packet of cigarettes just before arriving

—everything possible to give them a boost.

It usually takes a day or so before they come down to earth, then they become angry, irritable, and on edge. The first two weeks are critical. That's when they can't have a lot of outside contact; that's when their system is coming free of drugs. After that they can begin to take part in the general everyday life of the centre.

How do you check development and growth?
Lindsay: This is an area where we need a lot of discernment. We do have certain criteria, for instance their attitude to work—whether they are diligent or lazy, and their general demeanour—whether critical or co-operative.

Myk: How they handle money is important, once they start to carry responsibility. Some are devious, not handing back exact change, or not giving a full account of all money spent. How they handle conflict or a crisis is another. Many a promising man or woman has slipped back into drug addiction because some apparently insurmountable problem has thrown them back on to their old 'escape' route.

Lindsay: Another test is the sort of people to whom they relate. If a person prefers to hang round with new ones that's usually a bad sign. When they want to be with the converted ones, the ones that are spiritual, then that's a good indication that they are starting to have discernment. Another factor is their response to having responsibility. Many start to grow because for the first time in their lives someone is willing to trust them. Informal conversations can lead to good insights when we ask questions like, 'How are you coping with life here?' or 'Are you getting over such and such?'

266

What do government departments and social workers think about you?

Lindsay: In one town we have been received very kindly by the assistant mayor. He revoked an earlier decision asking us to leave. A factor that helps is that we are willing to take any person who is an addict or is depressed. Hospitals now ring us and ask us to take people when they have no place for them. Social workers will ask us to care for cases that no one else wants to help, such as a drug addict who had thrown himself through a window. He was in bad shape physically as well as being on drugs. No-one wanted him because he was in the terminal stage of AIDS. They asked us to come in and wash him every day. Our men went faithfully for quite some time before he was admitted to a hospice. That gave us real credibility.

The social workers who deal with drug addicts at the street level are warm towards us. But those who sit in their offices and write theses are very cold because they see us as a non-professional group; they are the ones that usually put the obstacles in our path.

5

THE THREE STAGES OF REHABILITATION
by Elliott Tepper

Our programme is simply the gospel. We preach the gospel, we live the gospel, and we introduce people to the spiritual benefits of the gospel which will inevitably bring change to all the dimensions of living.

In our presentations to the government and the public, we have delineated a three-stage programme. (In all honesty we really don't think of them as three stages; we just live Christ.)

But our first phase would be the detoxification of the individual, meeting the physical needs without trying to make him a Christian or obliging him to accept the Christian doctrine. We simply love him, receive him and create an environment where he can be rehabilitated. That involves total abstinence, which is the only answer for detoxification. Good food, rest, work, recreation and detoxification—that will bring a person around physically.

They will be on the right road within a month, but then the second phase begins with an emotional rehabilitation. It touches the soul life of the individual—the mind and the emotions.

By living in the community which has its own internal customs and structure, they are encouraged to rebuild their debilitated mental, moral and emotional lives in conformity to the collective personality of the Betel family.

They have to rise at a certain hour; they have to do their duties; they have to take care of their personal needs, their beds, their toiletries. They have to work in the kitchen or house; then they have to join a work team, work daily and give an account of their time.

We help them change habits, acting like resident parents for them. And of course with change of habit we trust their attitudes will change. This means acquiring a positive outlook on life, respecting authority, and respect for others.

But all that falls short if there's no new birth or regeneration. We have to make that bridge from the soul-life to the spirit, and that can only come through God.

We create a holy atmosphere, with daily devotions, regular meetings, preaching of the word and prayer times.

The staff, who are Christ-centred, create an environment where each man, in his own time and in his own way, can hear the gospel and make his own decision for Christ, repent of his past life, open his heart and receive the Holy Spirit. Of course between the soul and the spirit you have the heart, which is the bridge between the soul-life and the spirit-life, and that's where we relate to them—on an emotional and a spiritual level. Then of course there's sanctification. Once a person is born again and his spirit is renewed, God begins the whole process of renewal. The life of personal holiness starts to develop. Men begin to desire to be holy and then to apply the word to their lives. So in the second phase we touch the soul and the spirit.

During that time they're also trained in secular aspects of life. They join work teams; they might go to the auto shop and learn mechanics. We are not equipped to give them real professional training, but they work alongside other mechanics. They can work in the body shop; they can fix a car or paint it, or they'll learn how to paint a house. They might join a team doing plumbing. Again, we can't turn them into professional plumbers, but they certainly pick up skills that allow them to join a government programme or other apprenticeships.

Back to normal life

The third phase would be the re-insertion stage. Once they're physically detoxified, once their emotions, attitude and mind—their soul-life—have been renewed, and Christ is resident in their hearts, then they can function on a practical level, outside the community. But we feel we can let them go only when they manifest a stable personal relationship with God. That usually happens after about a year or two. We like to keep people for two or three years if possible, but after one year they are basically ready to go, provided they can return to a stable family environment or to a spouse who is a Christian, or to a local church—preferably all three, where they can be surrounded by love. If they don't have these, the odds are against them. They must enter the Christian subculture which is going to help insulate and protect them from the temptations of the world. Most churches are very glad to receive them because there's little church growth outside of work with drug addicts, and every convert is precious. So the pastors usually take good care of them.

Many of our people decide to stay on with us in the ministry. We have more than thirty couples now living and working full time with us, either in flats or in hostels that we maintain ourselves. They live normal lives; whilst living outside the community they minister inside. Most of the others go home and find work. They get jobs according to their qualifications. Our people are mainly from the working classes and do not have much education. They don't become lawyers or doctors, but they do become welders, mechanics and masons. They do the things they did before; they do them honestly and they do them well. We have some who have started their own businesses, like Paco Corrales who now has his own gas installation business. Luis Lopez is now a building contractor. Many others have gone out and found good jobs where they are working faithfully. Paco and Luis, for example, have even purchased their own houses and this is only a few years after being pulled out of the gutter. Many of our people are now doing very well.

Some people could criticise us and say that we bring young people just 90% of the way, that we have to keep them in the community to shore them up. We affirm that they are perfectly capable of functioning outside the fellowship, and most of them do, but we are pleased when some stay with us and participate in the ministry of the kingdom.

Frankly, I'd much rather have a church that functions as an army and is mobile and active. I want to have a church like the early Moravians with every member a missionary, or like the early Salvation Army, with every member a soldier, or like the Christian Missionary Alliance Society where one out of ten or twenty members becomes a missionary. I admire the Bethany Fellowship in Minneapolis where the whole early community was made up of those totally committed to the work, working in the Bethany business or going abroad as Bethany missionaries. I don't want a normal church. If that's a criticism, so be it. So our third phase would be setting them loose but knowing God and able to function, if necessary, independent of the community in normal life.

If according to the will of God, they want to continue as Betel members, extending the kingdom of God and extending the Betel vision to the nations, then we rejoice.

Stewart and Marie Dinnen have served with WEC
International since 1949. They have fulfilled several roles during this time; from 1984-87 Stewart
was International Secretary. They are currently
based in Tasmania, Australia.

For further information about BETEL contact
Mr E Tepper,
Calle Caspe 6,
28022 Madrid,
Spain

Further information about WEC INTERNATIONAL
can be obtained in the following countries:

Australia: 48 Woodside Ave, Strathfield, NSW 2138
Britain: Bulstrode, Oxford Road, Gerrards Cross, Bucks
SL9 8SZ
Canada: 37 Aberdeen Avenue, Hamilton, ON L8P-2N6

Hong Kong: PO Box 73261, Kowloon Central PO, Kowloon,
Hong Kong
New Zealand: PO Box 27264, MT Roskill, Auckland 1030

South Africa: PO Box 47777, Greyville 4023, Natal
Singapore: PO Box 185, Raffles City, Singapore 9117
USA: PO Box 1707, Fort Washington, PA 19034